AS/A-L

Richard Swan

The Miller's Prologue & Tale

Geoffrey Chaucer

Philip Allan Updates
Market Place
Deddington
Oxfordshire
OX15 0SE
Tel: 01869 338652
Fax: 01869 337590
e-mail: sales@philipallan.co.uk
www.philipallan.co.uk

© Philip Allan Updates 2005

ISBN-13 978-1-84489-206-8
ISBN-10 1-84489-206-9

Printed by Raithby, Lawrence & Co Ltd, Leicester

Environmental information
The paper on which this title is printed is sourced from mills using wood from managed, sustainable forests.

P00517

Contents

Introduction

Aims of the guide 2

Assessment Objectives 2

Revision advice 3

Writing examination essays 5

Text Guidance

Contexts

    Chaucer's life 10

    The medieval worldview 11

    Medieval society 14

    Medieval beliefs 16

    Tradition and innovation 18

    Chaucer and his contemporaries 19

    Pilgrimage 22

    Story collections 24

    Chaucer's audience and purpose 26

    The framework of *The Canterbury Tales* 29

    The multiple narrator in *The Canterbury Tales* 31

    Chaucer's verse 32

    Chaucer's language 34

The Miller in 'The General Prologue' 35

Making sense of the story 37

Characters 40

Themes 42

Humour 45

'The Miller's Tale' as a fabliau 47

The tale and its teller 48

Moral vision 49

Chaucer's narrative technique 51

Literary terms and concepts 53

Questions and Answers

Essay questions, specimen plans and notes 58

Sample essays 62

Further study 65

Introduction

Aims of the guide

The purpose of this Student Text Guide to 'The Miller's Prologue and Tale' is to enable you to organise your thoughts and responses to the text, to deepen your understanding of key features and aspects, and finally to help you to address the particular requirements of examination questions in order to obtain the best possible grade. It will also prove useful to those writing a coursework piece on the text. The guide contains a number of summaries, lists, analyses and references to help with the content and construction of essay assignments. References to the text are to the Cambridge University Press edition, edited by James Winny.

It is assumed that you have read and studied the text already under the guidance of a teacher or lecturer. This is a revision guide, not an introduction, although some of its content serves the purpose of providing initial background. It can be read in its entirety in one sitting, or it can be dipped into and used as a reference guide to specific and separate aspects of the text.

The remainder of this Introduction section consists of Assessment Objectives; a revision scheme which gives a suggested programme for using the material in the guide; and practical advice on writing essay answers.

The Text Guidance section consists of a series of subsections which examine key aspects of the text including contexts, interpretations and controversies. Emboldened terms within the Text Guidance section are glossed in 'literary terms and concepts' on pp. 53–56.

The final section, Questions and Answers, includes mark schemes, exemplar essay plans and examples of marked work.

Assessment Objectives

The Assessment Objectives (AOs) for A-level English Literature are common to all boards:

AO1	communicate clearly the knowledge, understanding and insight appropriate to literary study, using appropriate terminology and accurate and coherent written expression
AO2i	respond with knowledge and understanding to literary texts of different types and periods
AO2ii	respond with knowledge and understanding to literary texts of different types and periods, exploring and commenting on relationships and comparisons between literary texts

AO3	show detailed understanding of the ways in which writers' choices of form, structure and language shape meanings
AO4	articulate independent opinions and judgements, informed by different interpretations of literary texts by other readers
AO5i	show understanding of the contexts in which literary texts are written and understood
AO5ii	evaluate the significance of cultural, historical and other contextual influences on literary texts and study

A summary of each Assessment Objective is given below and would be worth memorising:

AO1	clarity of written communication
AO2	informed personal response in relation to time and genre (literary context)
AO3	the creative literary process (context of writing)
AO4	critical and interpretative response (context of reading)
AO5	evaluation of influences (cultural context)

It is essential that you pay close attention to the AOs, and their weighting, for the board for which you are entered. These are what the examiner will be looking for, and you must address them *directly* and *specifically*, in addition to proving general familiarity with and understanding of the text, and being able to present an argument clearly, relevantly and convincingly.

Remember that the examiners are seeking above all else evidence of an *informed personal response* to the text. A revision guide such as this can help you to understand the text and to form your own opinions, but it cannot replace your own ideas and responses as an individual reader.

Revision advice

For the examined units it is possible that either brief or more extensive revision will be necessary because the original study of the text took place some time previously. It is therefore useful to know how to go about revising and which tried and tested methods are considered the most successful for literature exams at all levels, from GCSE to degree finals.

Below is a guide on how not to do it — think of reasons why not in each case.

Don't:
- leave it until the last minute
- assume you remember the text well enough and don't need to revise at all

- spend hours designing a beautiful revision schedule
- revise more than one text at the same time
- think you don't need to revise because it is an open book exam
- decide in advance what you think the questions will be and revise only for those
- try to memorise particular essay plans
- reread texts randomly and aimlessly
- revise for longer than 2 hours in one sitting
- miss school lessons in order to work alone at home
- try to learn a whole ring-binder's worth of work
- rely on a study guide instead of the text

There are no short-cuts to effective exam revision; the only one way to know a text well, and to know your way around it in an exam, is to have done the necessary studying. If you use the following method, in six easy stages, for both open and closed book revision, you will not only revisit and reassess all your previous work on the text in a manageable way but will be able to distil, organise and retain your knowledge. Don't try to do it all in one go: take regular breaks for refreshment and a change of scene.

(1) Between a month and a fortnight before the exam, depending on your schedule (a simple list of stages with dates displayed in your room, not a work of art!), you will need to reread the text, this time taking stock of all the underlinings and marginal annotations as well. As you read, collect onto sheets of A4 the essential ideas and quotations as you come across them. The acts of selecting key material and recording it as notes are natural ways of stimulating thought and aiding memory.

(2) Reread the highlighted areas and marginal annotations in your critical extracts and background handouts, and add anything useful from them to your list of notes and quotations. Then reread your previous essays and the teacher's comments. As you look back through essays written earlier in the course, you should have the pleasant sensation of realising that you can now write much better on the text than you could then. You will also discover that much of your huge file of notes is redundant or repeated, and that you have changed your mind about some beliefs, so that the distillation process is not too daunting. Selecting what is important is the way to crystallise your knowledge and understanding.

(3) During the run-up to the exam you need to do lots of practice essay plans to help you identify any gaps in your knowledge and give you practice in planning in 5–8 minutes. Past paper titles for you to plan are provided in this guide, some of which can be done as full timed essays — and marked strictly according to exam criteria — which will show whether length and timing are problematic for you. If you have not seen a copy of a real exam paper before you take your first module, ask to see a past paper so that you are familiar with the layout and rubric.

(4) About a week before the exam, reduce your two or three sides of A4 notes to a double-sided postcard of very small, dense writing. Collect a group of keywords by once again selecting and condensing, and use abbreviations for quotations (first and last word), and character and place names (initials). (For the comparison unit your postcard will need to refer to key points, themes and quotations in both texts relevant to the specific theme or genre topic.) The act of choosing and writing out the short quotations will help you to focus on the essential issues, and to recall them quickly in the exam. Make sure that your selection covers the main themes and includes examples of symbolism, style, comments on character, examples of irony, point of view or other significant aspects of the text. Previous class discussion and essay writing will have indicated which quotations are useful for almost any title; pick those which can serve more than one purpose, for instance those which reveal character and theme, and are also an example of language. In this way a minimum number of quotations can have maximum application.

(5) You now have in a compact, accessible form all the material for any possible essay title. There are only half a dozen themes relevant to a literary text so if you have covered these, you should not meet with any nasty surprises when you read the exam questions. You don't need to refer to your file of paperwork again, or even to the text. For the few days before the exam, you can read through your handy postcard whenever and wherever you get the opportunity. Each time you read it, which will only take a few minutes, you are reminding yourself of all the information you will be able to recall in the exam to adapt to the general title or to support an analysis of particular passages.

(6) A fresh, active mind works wonders, and information needs time to settle, so don't try to cram just before the exam. Relax the night before and get a good night's sleep. Then you will be able to enter the exam room with all the confidence of a well-prepared candidate.

Writing examination essays

Essay content

One of the key skills you are being asked to demonstrate at A-level is the ability to select and tailor your knowledge of the text and its background to the question set in the exam paper. In order to reach the highest levels, you need to avoid 'pre-packaged' essays which lack focus, relevance and coherence, and which simply contain everything you know about the text. Be ruthless in rejecting irrelevant material, after considering whether it can be made relevant by a change of emphasis. Aim to cover the whole question, not just part of it; your response

needs to demonstrate breadth and depth, covering the full range of text elements: character, event, theme and language. Only half a dozen approaches are possible for any set text, though they may be phrased in a variety of ways, and they are likely to refer to the key themes of the text. Preparation of the text therefore involves extensive discussion and practice at manipulating these core themes so that there should be no surprises in the exam. An apparently new angle is more likely to be something familiar presented in an unfamiliar way and you should not panic or reject the choice of question because you think you know nothing about it.

Exam titles are open-ended in the sense that there is not an obvious right answer, and you would therefore be unwise to give a dismissive, extreme or entirely one-sided response. The question would not have been set if the answer were not debatable. An ability and willingness to see both sides is an Assessment Objective and shows independence of judgement as a reader. Don't be afraid to explore the issues and don't try to tie the text into one neat interpretation. If there is ambiguity, it is likely to be deliberate on the part of the author and must be discussed; literary texts are complex and often paradoxical, and it would be a misreading of them to suggest that there is only one possible interpretation. You are not expected, however, to argue equally strongly or extensively for both sides of an argument, since personal opinion is an important factor. It is advisable to deal with the alternative view at the beginning of your response, and then construct your own view as the main part of the essay. This makes it less likely that you will appear to cancel out your own line of argument.

Choosing the right question

The first skill you must show when presented with the exam paper is the ability to choose the better, for you, of the two questions on your text where there is a choice. This is not to say that you should always go for the same type of essay (whole-text or extract-based), and if the question is not one which you feel happy with for any reason, you should seriously consider the other, even if it is not the type you normally prefer. It is unlikely but possible that a question contains a word you are not sure you know the meaning of, in which case it would be safer to choose the other one.

Don't be tempted to choose a question because of its similarity to one you have already done. Freshness and thinking on the spot usually produce a better product than attempted recall of a previous essay which may have received only a mediocre mark in the first place. The exam question is unlikely to have exactly the same focus and your response may seem 'off centre' as a result, as well as stale and perfunctory in expression. Essay questions fall into the following categories: close section analysis and relation to whole text; characterisation; setting and atmosphere; structure and effectiveness; genre;

language and style; themes and issues. Remember, however, that themes are relevant to all essays and that analysis, not just description, is always required.

Once you have decided which exam question to attempt, follow the procedure below for whole-text and passage-based, open- and closed-book essays.

(1) Underline all the key words in the question and note how many parts the question has.

(2) Plan your answer, using aspects of the key words and parts of the question as sub-headings, in addition to themes. Aim for 10–12 ideas. Check that the Assessment Objectives are covered.

(3) Support your argument by selecting the best examples of characters, events, imagery and quotations to prove your points. Remove ideas for which you can find no evidence.

(4) Structure your answer by grouping and numbering your points in a logical progression. Identify the best general point to keep for the conclusion.

(5) Introduce your essay with a short paragraph setting the context and defining the key words in the question as broadly, but relevantly, as possible.

(6) Write the rest of the essay, following your structured plan but adding extra material if it occurs to you. Paragraph your writing and consider expression, especially sentence structure and vocabulary choices, as you write. Signal changes in the direction of your argument with paragraph openers such as 'Furthermore' and 'However'. Use plenty of short, integrated quotations and use the words of the text rather than your own where possible. Use technical terms appropriately, and write concisely and precisely, avoiding vagueness and ambiguity.

(7) Your conclusion should sound conclusive and make it clear that you have answered the question. It should be an overview of the question and the text, not a repetition or a summary of points already made.

(8) Cross out your plan with a neat, diagonal line.

(9) Check your essay for content, style, clarity and accuracy. With neat crossings-out, correct errors of fact, spelling, grammar and punctuation. Improve expression if possible, and remove any repetition and irrelevance. Add clarification and missing evidence, if necessary, using omission marks or asterisks. Even at this stage, good new material can be added.

There is no such thing as a perfect or model essay; flawed essays can gain full marks. There is always something more which could have been said, and examiners realise that students have limitations when writing under pressure in timed conditions. You

are not penalised for what you didn't say in comparison to some idealised concept of the answer, but rewarded for the knowledge and understanding you have shown. It is not as difficult as you may think to do well, provided that you are familiar with the text and have sufficient essay-writing experience. If you follow the above process and **underline, plan, support, structure, write** and **check**, you can't go far wrong.

Contexts

This guide is designed to help you make sense of 'The Miller's Prologue and Tale' both in relation to its parent work, *The Canterbury Tales*, and in its historical and cultural context. For this reason, reference is made throughout the guide to *The Canterbury Tales* as a whole and to 'The General Prologue' in particular, which you should read in detail as background to 'The Miller's Prologue and Tale'.

Assessment Objective 5 requires the candidate to 'evaluate the significance of cultural, historical and other contextual influences on literary texts'. There are a number of contexts in which 'The Miller's Prologue and Tale' can be viewed.

Chaucer's life

Although nothing is known about Chaucer as a person, and almost nothing about his private life, he was a prominent figure in the second half of the fourteenth century, with associations and positions at court. He served under three kings, and was entrusted by Edward III with foreign journeys handling the king's secret affairs. The public aspects of his life are therefore well documented, and demonstrate that he would have had direct experience of nearly all the kinds of people he represents in *The Canterbury Tales*.

There are some uncertainties and some periods of Chaucer's life for which little is known, but the salient dates are outlined below. The approximate dates for the composition of his literary works are also given.

Key dates and works

c. 1340–45	Geoffrey Chaucer born, son of a London wine merchant.
1357	Becomes a page in the household of the Countess of Ulster.
1360	Captured while serving in France; ransomed by Edward III.
1366	Journeys to Spain; marries Philippa Rouet around this time.
1367	Appointed Yeoman of the Chamber in the king's household.
1367–77	Journeys abroad on the king's business.
1369	Campaigns in France; appointed Esquire in the king's household.
Pre-1372	*The Book of the Duchess*.
1372–73	First journey to Italy.
1372–80	*The House of Fame*.
1374	Appointed Comptroller of Customs and Subsidy.
1377	Edward III dies; accession of Richard II.
1378	Second journey to Italy.
1380–86	*The Parliament of Fowls*; *Troilus and Criseyde*; *The Legend of Good Women*.

1385	Appointed Justice of the Peace for Kent.
1385–1400	*The Canterbury Tales.*
1386	Sits in Parliament as Knight of the Shire for Kent.
1389	Appointed Clerk to the King's Works.
1391	Appointed Subforester.
1394	Awarded extra grant for good service.
1399	Richard II deposed; accession of Henry IV.
	Previous grants confirmed by Henry IV.
1400	Dies on 25 October; buried in Westminster Abbey.

The medieval worldview

The worldview that would have been shared by Chaucer and his European contemporaries was markedly different from that of today, and you need to gain an understanding of it if you are to make proper sense of Chaucer's writings. Much of the information that follows was automatic knowledge for any medieval person, and so explicit references to it rarely occur.

The physical universe

The universe had been created by God, and was finite, comprehensible and purposeful; it existed as a home for man. Every element could be explained and every element was interrelated, so that the place and functioning of one aspect of the universe could be understood within the operation of the whole structure.

The Ptolemaic system

The cosmological model accepted in the medieval period is known as the Ptolemaic system, being a refinement of the ideas propounded by the Egyptian astronomer Ptolemy in the second century AD. This model held sway for well over 1,000 years, and was only superseded by more modern models based on the Copernican system long after the end of the Middle Ages.

According to the Ptolemaic system, the universe consisted of nine concentric transparent crystal spheres, with the Earth at the centre. Each of the first seven spheres contained a planet: in order, the Moon, Mercury, Venus, the Sun, Mars, Jupiter and Saturn. The eighth sphere contained the fixed stars. The ninth sphere, the so-called *primum mobile* (prime mover), contained no planet of its own, but its motion imparted movement to all the other spheres. God, who existed outside the created universe, controlled the whole process. The universe was therefore thought to be a clock-like mechanism, and the sound made by the mechanism could be imagined, or in certain exceptional circumstances heard. This was the famed 'music of the spheres', a divine harmony that inspired many writers, artists and musicians.

Heaven was thought to be the area outside the created universe, which yields the idea of going 'up' to heaven. Heaven itself was unaffected by time, movement or change. Between the *primum mobile* and the Moon there was movement but no decay or change; everything was perfect and divine. Change was limited to events within the sphere of the Moon, and therefore on Earth. This explained weather systems, the atmosphere, and the whole idea of human life being sub-lunar — literally, below the Moon. Events on Earth were affected by the movement of all the spheres — hence belief in astrology — but events taking place on Earth itself only affected the universe as far as the Moon. The deaths of Julius Caesar and King Duncan in Shakespeare's plays, for example, therefore cause chaos in the natural world and in the skies. The Moon, being the closest planet to Earth, had the most influence on human affairs, which explains why 'lunatics' were thought of as being directly affected by the Moon. Hell, rather neatly, found its place at the centre of the Earth, simultaneously suggesting the idea of going 'down' to Hell and meaning that Hell was at the furthest possible remove from Heaven.

The Great Chain of Being

Parallel to the physical order in the structure of the universe was the logical order implied by the medieval belief in hierarchy. The system by which everything on Earth was believed to be organised is generally known as the Great Chain of Being. This categorised all of the items in the universe, with God at the top and inanimate matter at the bottom. The table below shows this hierarchy and the associated properties of each item.

Item	Properties
God	Reason, Movement, Life, Existence
Angels	Reason, Movement, Life, Existence
Man	Reason, Movement, Life, Existence
Animals	Movement, Life, Existence
Plants	Life, Existence
Inanimate matter	Existence

The hierarchy was governed by the universal principle that it is the duty of each creature to obey those higher up the hierarchy, and the responsibility of each creature to govern those below it. This gives rise to some important observations. First, it is the duty of all creatures to obey God. Equally, it is God's duty to govern his universe responsibly. Mankind was created 'in God's image', which means possessing the same attributes; it is the faculty of reason that sets humans apart from all other creatures on Earth. It is the duty of mankind to obey God and the messages conveyed by his angels; it is the responsibility of mankind to govern the Earth in accordance with God's wishes.

As with the universe itself, once this system is understood a large number of things make sense. The Fall of Man, the original sin when Adam and Eve disobeyed God (symbolically by eating an apple), entailed a fundamental violation of the Great Chain of Being, and it is no surprise that its consequences were therefore absolute. Genesis makes clear that their sin was to disrupt the hierarchy by believing themselves to be higher than they were — they fell prey to the devil's temptation that they would be 'as Gods, knowing good and evil'. Satan himself fell from heaven because of the same sin of pride, believing himself equal to God when his duty was to obey his natural superior. In the opposite direction, a medieval person would utterly condemn animal rights supporters for failure to understand the hierarchy. Over the last few centuries this sense of vertical hierarchy has been dismantled, so that many people no longer recognise a deity that is 'above' them, and equally refuse to claim superiority over creatures notionally 'below' them.

Hierarchies within the groups

Within each part of the hierarchy, further hierarchies existed, giving rise to the concept of 'degree' — one's exact positioning on the social scale. There was a hierarchy within the animals, which is why the lion is still often referred to as the 'king' of the beasts. Among human beings, several such hierarchies were visible. In secular society, the king was the sole ruler, followed by the nobility (themselves with several ranks) and then the rest; even among the peasants there were various gradings depending on their conditions of service or tenure. The parallel structure in the Church had the pope as the supreme authority, and a number of ranks from cardinal, archbishop and bishop down to parish priest and curate. In every case the same governing rule applied, which is why kings and popes could claim divine sanction for their rule and why regicide was viewed with such horror.

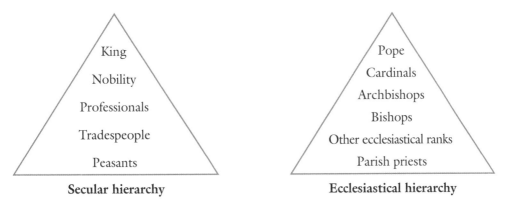

Secular hierarchy

King
Nobility
Professionals
Tradespeople
Peasants

Ecclesiastical hierarchy

Pope
Cardinals
Archbishops
Bishops
Other ecclesiastical ranks
Parish priests

The tension between the two hierarchies caused problems, most famously in the case of Thomas Becket. A friend and chancellor to Henry II, Becket was appointed by

the king as Archbishop of Canterbury. Henry hoped that this would give him power over the Church, but Becket defied him and claimed that ecclesiastical authority was higher than secular authority. This led to Becket's assassination in 1170, and the start of the veneration of him as a saint that made Canterbury the leading pilgrimage site in England.

The final significant hierarchical distinction, and the one with the most far-reaching implications for Western society and history, was the claim that men were hierarchically superior to women, a doctrine founded on Genesis. This meant that men could and should rule over women, and women had to obey their husbands. Until recently, the standard Christian marriage service included the vow that the wife would obey the husband, but without the reciprocal promise of obedience from the man. Centuries of institutionalised inequality and anti-feminism were an automatic concomitant of such a belief, the repercussions of which are still felt today.

However, despite this notion of the relative status of men and women, the situation in reality was always more complex. Debate over the relative status, rights and responsibilities of men and women was as rife in Chaucer's time as it is today. There was a large corpus of antifeminist writing because most writers were male clerics, but it is clear that women were far from silent, as Chaucer reveals in his portrayal of the Wife of Bath. Much of *The Canterbury Tales* is concerned with this topic, with all kinds of relationships and attitudes being portrayed, and it is noticeable that in 'The Miller's Tale' Alison is an active and central figure in the narrative.

Medieval society

The three estates model

Medieval society comprised three classes or estates: those who fought, those who prayed, and those who laboured to sustain the first two groups. In principle, this was the basis of feudal society, although the reality was never that simple.

The first estate was the clergy, a large group that maintained the fabric of society through the service of God and the regulation of human affairs. The second estate was the nobility, who were few in number, and were landowners and professional soldiers. The third estate was the vast bulk of ordinary people, who were subject to the laws of both the other groups. In a primarily agrarian society, this group comprised mainly peasants who laboured on the land to create the food and wealth by which society was sustained. A person was born into either the second or third estate, and might enter the first (the clergy) through vocation or for a variety of other reasons, including a desire for security or advancement. Otherwise, people were expected to remain in the rank to which God had allocated them at birth.

In addition to being members of one of the three estates, medieval women were also placed in three categories: virgin, wife and widow. They were thus sometimes thought of as a separate, fourth estate, inferior in consequence and importance to men.

In practice, the structure of medieval society was not as simplistic as the three estates model suggests, and by Chaucer's lifetime significant changes had taken place. From the start, there were inequalities in the third estate, which necessarily covered a vast range of occupations. With the passing of time people strove to better their conditions, and by the fourteenth century there were numerous distortions and anomalies within the system. The range of characters in *The Canterbury Tales* illustrates this. The only members of the nobility are the Knight and his son the Squire. The only true peasant is the Ploughman. There are several members of the clergy, but only three women. The remaining pilgrims all occupy a shifting middle ground; they are technically members of the third estate, but to equate the Man of Law — a wealthy, influential professional — with the Miller is clearly absurd. Although class distinctions continue to exist to this day, it is evident that the feudal division into classes had already lost much of its practical significance long before the end of the Middle Ages; *The Canterbury Tales* amply shows how there was a blurring of position, wealth and influence in this period.

Social change

The late fourteenth century was a time of great change, which makes *The Canterbury Tales* a valuable window onto an important period in English history.

The Black Death

The catalyst for change was the outbreak of the plague known as the Black Death. This swept through Europe and devastated England on several occasions in the fourteenth century, most radically in 1348–49, early in Chaucer's life. The exact figures are unknown, but estimates suggest that up to 40% of England's population died. The effects of this were colossal. Before the mid-fourteenth century, the population had been expanding, meaning that labour was plentiful and land use was intensive. Afterwards, labour became scarcer, but pressures on land decreased. Thousands of individual jobs and roles were lost. Inevitably, there was suddenly scope for enterprising people from all ranks of society to seek better conditions and better occupations.

The Peasants' Revolt

Social unrest was a likely outcome of social change, and it is not surprising that the uprising known as the Peasants' Revolt occurred in 1381. This rebellion was primarily triggered by increased taxation, and resulted in a march on the city of London and demands for the eradication of serfdom. The rebellion gained little of immediate consequence, but it offers an important insight into the way that society

was changing at a rapid pace. At the time, Chaucer was living above Aldgate, one of the six city gates of London, so he must have had an intimate awareness of the events that took place.

Language

Further changes were probably hastened by the upheaval following the outbreaks of plague. It was during Chaucer's lifetime that English re-emerged as the official language of court and the law, supplanting the Norman French that William the Conqueror had imposed and paving the way for the dominance of what would become Modern English in the nation and beyond. This is reflected in Chaucer's choice of English for all his major works; by comparison, his friend John Gower wrote three major works, one in English, one in French and one in Latin.

The Church

Although it remained a paramount power both in politics and in society, the Church was also subject to upheaval at this time. In 1378, one of the years in which Chaucer visited Italy, the Great Schism took place. This was a rift in the Church which resulted in the election of two popes — an unimaginable situation if one considers the hierarchical significance of the pope as the appointed representative of God on Earth. The Italians had elected Urban VI as pope, but the French, supported by their king, Charles V, appointed Clement VII, who set up his throne in Avignon. Like the Peasants' Revolt, the Great Schism led to further questioning of the authority of established powers, and a greater willingness on the part of ordinary people to press their own claims for rights and privileges.

In England the effects of the upheaval in the Church were particularly felt in the work of John Wycliffe (1328–84), a reformer who attacked papal authority and denounced the Great Schism as 'Antichrist itself'. He argued that every man had the right to examine the Bible for himself, and sponsored the first translation of the Bible into English. He was a major figure in the latter part of the fourteenth century, and his work led to the heretical movement known as Lollardy. It is debatable whether or not Chaucer had Lollard sympathies; certainly his writing, in particular in *The Canterbury Tales*, attacks abuses within the Church in a way with which Wycliffe would have sympathised.

Medieval beliefs

The seven deadly sins

One of the most common and enduring aspects of medieval religious imagery is its focus on the seven deadly sins, references to which are still found in modern times, long after direct belief in such a system has faded. There is occasional variation in

the list of sins, but this is the most common and is listed in the order in which they appear in 'The Parson's Tale':

English	Latin
Pride	Superbia
Envy	Invidia
Anger (wrath)	Ira
Sloth	Accidia
Avarice (greed)	Avaricia
Gluttony	Gula
Lust (lechery)	Luxuria

Pride is traditionally the chief of the sins because it incorporates all the others. It involves a false belief in one's own importance, and is the sin through which Lucifer fell and became Satan, and through which Adam and Eve fell, tempted to believe that they could be 'as gods'. Pride in one's opinion could lead to anger; pride in one's personal attributes could lead to lust.

Although occasional attempts have been made to demonstrate that the whole scheme of *The Canterbury Tales* is an exposition on the seven deadly sins, it is more fruitful to see them as an underlying part of medieval belief, and one which colours many of the portraits and the stories in *The Canterbury Tales*. Sometimes the symbolism is evident. The Wife of Bath's unrestrained sexual desire makes her guilty of lechery; the Monk is guilty of gluttony, because of his unrestrained desire for physical well-being; the Pardoner is avaricious. In other cases the particular sin of a character is more arguable; a harsh judgement of the Prioress would make her guilty of pride, whereas a more charitable one would accuse her of greed, the desire for worldly goods and status. The Merchant, who is 'Sowninge alwey th'encrees of his winning' ('The General Prologue', line 277), is a more obvious example of monetary avarice.

The four humours

Medieval science held that all matter was composed of four **elements**, each with its associated qualities, which in turn gave rise to a human disposition known as the humour or temper. It was believed that different **humours** were predominant in individuals, dictating their temperament or 'complexioun', and that sickness arose when the balance of the humours was disturbed (an idea which survives in the modern phrase 'to be in a bad temper'). The qualities of each element, and the humour it was thought to cause, are given in the table below.

Element	Qualities	Humour	Personality
Earth	Cold and dry	Melancholy	Melancholic
Air	Hot and moist	Blood (sanguinity)	Sanguine (cheerful)
Fire	Hot and dry	Choler	Angry
Water	Cold and moist	Phlegm	Phlegmatic (unemotional)

Belief in the four humours was so ingrained in medieval society that it rarely receives specific treatment, but its consequences can be seen in a number of Chaucer's pilgrims in 'The General Prologue'. The Reeve is 'a sclendre colerik man' (line 589), his hot and dry nature having wasted his flesh away so that he is stick-like. The Franklin is also precisely identified: 'Of his complexioun he was sangwin' (line 335). The Wife of Bath has the ruddy complexion of a sanguine character too: 'Boold was hir face, and fair, and reed of hewe' (line 460). The Doctor's expertise (lines 421–23) is based on his understanding of the humours and his ability to diagnose and prescribe accordingly:

> He knew the cause of everich maladie,
> Were it of hoot, or coold, or moist, or drie,
> And where they engendred, and of what humour.

It is amusing that modern students of social behaviour often try to reduce personality to a schematic interpretation — sometimes even featuring four 'types' — that is little different from the medieval scheme.

Tradition and innovation

When reading Chaucer, it is essential to understand the different attitude to innovation that distinguishes the medieval period from the modern age. Nowadays, the emphasis in artistic creation is on originality; a writer or other artist who deliberately copies another, even with modifications, is guilty of plagiarism. Students are well aware of the dangers and the penalties incurred by including plagiarism in their essays.

In the Middle Ages, the reverse was true. Originality was viewed with extreme suspicion, while adherence to what was traditional, established and accepted was applauded. It is easier to understand this attitude by taking the medieval worldview into account. God had created the universe, the Bible was the word of God, the Earth had been created for mankind, and while men and women obeyed God all was well. Everything about the world was established and fixed; the purpose of art and learning was not to discover 'new' things, but to reveal the glory and majesty of God's creation. Science, in so far as it existed at all, had the same aim.

Authorities

This attitude towards innovation helps to explain the medieval insistence on authorities — 'auctoritees' in Middle English. One could not rely on one's own opinion or judgement; instead, it was necessary to justify points by reference to accepted and established authorities. Inevitably the Bible, as the revealed word of God, was the ultimate and prime authority, closely followed by the writings of the early Church

fathers, including Augustine, Jerome, Tertullian and Gregory, all of whom feature heavily in Chaucer's works. However, almost any written authority that had survived from former times was likely to be taken up and quoted as occasion served, and it is common to find classical and Arabic sources, such as Ptolemy's *Almagest*, quoted as freely as Christian ones. 'The Merchant's Tale' offers a clear insight into the variety and importance of authorities in medieval literature.

The writer's task was not therefore to invent new things, but to take traditional and established tales and retell them in fresh and entertaining ways. In the same way that modern folk singers are not expected to create new pieces but to offer a personal interpretation of traditional songs, so medieval artists were more highly valued when they were reusing material with which their audience would already have been familiar. Most of Chaucer's stories in *The Canterbury Tales* were well known; it is significant that where he does seem to have invented a story, as is the case in 'The Franklin's Tale', he claims that it is just a translation. The skill of the artist was in his personal interpretation and presentation of the material, and in this Chaucer excelled.

Chaucer and his contemporaries

Chaucer's place in the history of English literature

It was John Dryden in the seventeenth century who labelled Chaucer 'the father of English poetry'. The modern reader may share this belief, because Chaucer is the earliest writer who is still widely known. His language is the most accessible, and the most 'modern', of all the medieval authors, and his emphasis on apparently realistic characters and themes seems modern too. He championed the use of the **iambic pentameter** and the rhyming couplet in much of his work, and this **metre** became the staple of English verse for the next 500 years. He was well known both in his own lifetime and after; many writers, including Shakespeare, were influenced by him and used his work as a source. The term 'father of English poetry' thus contains considerable truth, but it is also a distortion and conceals facts of which the student of Chaucer needs to be aware.

Chaucer died 600 years ago in 1400. *Beowulf*, the earliest known masterpiece in English, was composed around AD 700. By that reckoning, Chaucer lived more than half way through the chronological history of English literature and represents part of a continuing tradition rather than being the inventor of a new one.

It is easy to explain both the error contained in the popular view of Chaucer and his pre-eminence. First, there is the matter of language. *Beowulf* was composed in Anglo-Saxon (also known as Old English), and even Chaucer's great contemporaries,

such as William Langland and the anonymous author of *Sir Gawain and the Green Knight*, were writing in a style that dated back nearly 1,000 years. This was the so-called 'alliterative style', in which **alliteration** and a flexible rhythm were used to give lines shape and structure. In contrast, Chaucer wrote in a newfangled style influenced by French and Italian, using a set metre (mainly iambic pentameter in *The Canterbury Tales*) and rhyming couplets. His language was that used in London, and since London was the capital of England it was inevitable that Chaucer's language would be that which has come to predominate, and is therefore most familiar to subsequent generations. Moreover, until Chaucer's day there was very little 'literature' at all, in the sense of material that was ever written down. In a largely illiterate society, most culture was communicated orally, and written versions (including *Beowulf* itself) are fortuitous historical accidents. Most writing was done in Latin, the language of the educated (which essentially meant monks), and it is only from Chaucer's time onwards that there is a strong tradition of literature written in English.

Other works

Chaucer did not just write *The Canterbury Tales*. His other major work is *Troilus and Criseyde*, an 8,200-line poem written in a **metre** known as rhyme royal, a 7-line stanza in iambic pentameter, which he used in 'The Clerk's Tale' and 'The Prioress's Tale'. It is a tragic love story based on a supposed incident in the Trojan War; Chaucer borrowed the plot from Boccaccio, and it was later treated by Shakespeare and Dryden.

Chaucer also wrote a number of short verses, and several long poems of the type known as 'dream visions', in which the narrator falls asleep and dreams the events the poem relates. His interest in the status and role of women, a noticeable theme in *The Canterbury Tales*, is confirmed by *The Legend of Good Women*, which tells the stories of nine classical heroines, including Cleopatra and Thisbe.

Chaucer is famed for his wide reading and considerable education, which are illustrated by the fact that a number of his works are translations. He may have translated part of the *Roman de la Rose*, the vast thirteenth-century French poem that is a major source for and influence on Chaucer's own work; he specifically mentions it in 'The Merchant's Tale'. He translated from Latin *The Consolation of Philosophy* by Boethius, one of the best-known philosophical works in the Middle Ages (although it dates from the sixth century). Finally, he translated a scientific work, *A Treatise on the Astrolabe* (an instrument for measuring the position of the stars), which demonstrates the breadth of Chaucer's knowledge as well as confirming the interest in astrology visible throughout his work, for example in the description of the Doctor of Physic in 'The General Prologue', and the detail of Nicholas's learning in 'The Miller's Tale'.

Influences

A man as widely read as Chaucer would be familiar with all the great historical writers known in his time, together with many contemporaries. In addition, Chaucer's foreign travels on the king's business would have brought him into direct contact with the works of great European writers such as Boccaccio and Petrarch. Boccaccio's *Decameron* became a direct model for *The Canterbury Tales*. Chaucer was heavily influenced by biblical and religious writings, and by French and Italian writers of his own and previous centuries. It is worth thinking of him as a European rather than as a primarily English writer.

Numerous influences and sources, both general and specific, have been identified, and you should consult the edition of your text to appreciate the wealth of material on which Chaucer draws.

Contemporaries

Chaucer is the best known of the fourteenth-century writers, but during this period there was a huge flowering of writing in English. This was probably because English was re-emerging as the official language of the country after three centuries of Norman French domination, and because greater education and literacy allowed the production of true literature, i.e work that was composed in writing rather than orally.

In Chaucer's own lifetime there were two other major English writers whose importance rivals that of Chaucer — William Langland and the Gawain-poet.

Langland

William Langland wrote the great poem *Piers Plowman*. He was obsessed with the work and wrote three versions of it, ranging from 2,500 to 7,300 lines, over a period of 30 or 40 years. It is written in the **alliterative** style, a completely different form of poetry from Chaucer's, and one which was a development of Anglo-Saxon verse. *Piers Plowman* is a vast allegorical work in which Piers begins as the figure of a humble ploughman (comparable to the Ploughman of 'The General Prologue') and ends up as an allegorical representation of Christ. It is deeply serious, complex, and unique.

The Gawain-poet

Meanwhile, perhaps in Cheshire, there was a poet to whom authorship of all four of the poems preserved in the *Pearl* manuscript is usually attributed. The poet's name is not known, but he is most commonly referred to as the Gawain-poet, after his most famous work, *Sir Gawain and the Green Knight*. Like *Piers Plowman*, this poem is written in an **alliterative** verse form, but its language is now so unfamiliar that it is usually read in a modernised version. It tells the story of a mysterious Green Knight who challenges King Arthur's court to a 'game' at Christmas. He invites someone to chop his head off, but when Gawain does so the Green Knight calmly

collects his head and demands the right to return the blow in a year's time. The rest of the poem follows Gawain's dilemmas and tests as he seeks to keep his side of the bargain. The poem is a powerful, complex work that manages to be simultaneously humane and witty, profoundly moral and symbolic.

As well as these two writers there was John Gower, a personal friend of Chaucer's and a major influence on him, but whose works are no longer held in such esteem. He is best known for his *Confessio Amantis*.

The existence of these writers points to a vernacular tradition of enormous richness, variety and substance of which only a small portion has survived into the modern age. As well as Langland, the Gawain-poet and Gower, there was a wealth of material in all forms (poetry, drama and religious prose) that shows how Chaucer was part of a great age of literary output, rather than an isolated and unique genius.

Pilgrimage

The Canterbury Tales is based on two great defining structures: the story collection and the pilgrimage. The latter serves two purposes in the work. First, it is a **narrative** device, and second, it has a **thematic** function.

Narrative device

The role of pilgrimage in framing the narrative is simple but important. It gives Chaucer a basic plot — 30 pilgrims travel from London to Canterbury and back again — within which he can set out the multiple and varied narratives of his characters. It allows him to gather together a complete cross-section of the social hierarchy (excluding royalty, who would have travelled separately, and the very lowest serfs, who would not have been able to leave their work), in circumstances in which the characters can mingle on terms of near equality. This equality would have existed as regards their journey and experiences, but crucially there is equality of opportunity; every pilgrim gets the chance to tell a story, and every story receives the same attention, although what the pilgrims choose to do with their opportunities is another matter. The pilgrimage is also dynamic, so that circumstances on the journey can impinge on the storytelling framework, as happens when the pilgrims encounter a canon whose yeoman tells a tale of his own.

Thematic function

The second function of the pilgrimage in *The Canterbury Tales* is even more important. A pilgrimage has two aspects: it is a journey, but it is also a sacred journey. Both elements are crucial to an understanding of Chaucer's work.

Journeys

The image of the journey has always been central to human understanding. Life itself is conventionally seen as a journey from birth to death, and so any physical journey can be viewed as an image of life, with the travellers gaining experience as they progress. A pilgrimage is a special kind of physical journey, where the goal is a holy or sacred place. The parallel with the journey of life gains an extra significance, because the pilgrimage's sacred purpose is the equivalent of the soul's journey through life towards God. The best-known form of pilgrimage in modern times is the Muslim pilgrimage to Mecca, a journey that every devout Muslim is supposed to undertake at least once.

Holy sites and shrines

In the Middle Ages the pilgrimage was a common and popular activity and there were innumerable holy places to visit. The most holy site of all was Jerusalem, which the Wife of Bath visited three times, and Chaucer also mentions some of the other most famous ones, particularly Santiago de Compostela in Spain. In England, the shrine of Thomas Becket in Canterbury was the most popular destination following Becket's assassination in 1170, and it would remain so until it was destroyed by Henry VIII in the 1530s.

The importance of shrines lay in people's belief in the efficacy of saints and holy relics, as is evident from Chaucer's portrayal of the Pardoner. The Catholic Church taught that God could not be approached directly; it was therefore necessary to pray to those closest to him to intercede. Along with the Virgin Mary, with her unique position as the mother of Christ, the saints were thought to be endowed with special powers and influence. The relics of saints, particularly their bones, were held to have mystical, almost magical powers, and there were dozens of shrines associated with particular saints, each usually venerated for a specific quality.

Travel

Pilgrimage therefore held an important place in medieval life, but it was also a way to travel. In an insecure world, there was safety in numbers as well as the pleasure of company. Some of Chaucer's pilgrims, such as the Guildsmen, would be delighted to have a knight as part of the group, because he could offer practical as well as symbolic protection. A woman like the Wife of Bath would be pleased that the Guildsmen themselves were there, among whom she might look for her sixth husband; it would also have been difficult for her as a woman to travel alone.

It has been said that medieval pilgrimages were the equivalent of modern package holidays, and there is some value in the **analogy**, at least if it is seen as indicating the impulse to travel and the willingness of diverse people to band together for convenience and economies of scale. The comparison falls down, however, when the purpose of travel is considered. Modern holidaymakers largely

seek pleasure, and few travel with an overtly spiritual purpose. The reverse was true in the Middle Ages; although a few of Chaucer's pilgrims might have purely social or secular motives for the journey, most would have a greater or lesser degree of devotion, and all would have been aware of the sacred significance of their journey, even if they sometimes chose to ignore it.

Symbolism

Every character, every tale, and every word of *The Canterbury Tales* is contained within the symbolic framework of the pilgrimage, whether the individual characters are aware of it or not. When the Parson tells his tale of sin and repentance the connection is obvious, but the symbolism of the pilgrimage is equally relevant when the Merchant is telling his tale of an ill-judged marriage, when the Miller and the Reeve are trading tales at each other's expense, or when the Pardoner tries to con his audience through the techniques that he has just exposed. Every one of these is measured against, and judged by, the sacred context in which their journey and their lives take place.

The route to Canterbury

The map shows the details of the pilgrimage in *The Canterbury Tales*, including the places mentioned by Chaucer in the text. The journey from London to Canterbury was nearly 60 miles long and would usually have taken several days in each direction.

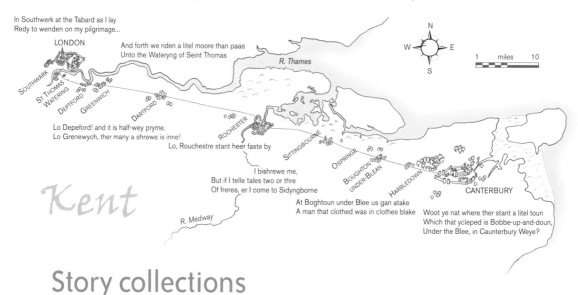

Story collections

In the Middle Ages, storytelling was a common form of communal entertainment. Literacy was scarce, and tales were told and retold, handed down from storyteller to storyteller through generations and centuries. Originally, almost all stories would have been in verse as this made them easier to remember, but as the Middle Ages

progressed an increasing number were written in prose. Traditional stories might be gathered together by a scribe, and gradually individual storytellers emerged who adapted material to their own designs and added to it. Collections of stories therefore became common, some of which were mere agglomerations of tales, and others unified and written by a single author. A few of these collections are still well known, the most familiar example being *The Thousand and One Nights*.

Influences and contemporary examples

Chaucer would have been influenced by two particular works. The anonymous *Gesta Romanorum* was an amorphous and disparate group of tales gathered in various forms over a long period, but united by a single guiding principle. The tales, many of them traditional or legendary, were viewed as **allegories**, that is to say literal narratives that could be given a parallel spiritual interpretation. Each tale is followed by an explanation offering a Christian reading of the text. For example, the classical tale of Atalanta, the swift runner who is beaten by a competitor who throws golden apples to distract her from the race, is seen as an allegory of the human soul being tempted by the devil. It is worth considering how far *The Canterbury Tales* can similarly be seen as a diverse group of stories unified by an underlying Christian message. The *Gesta Romanorum* is also a vital reminder that medieval literature could be complex, and that medieval audiences expected multiple and concealed meanings in a work of art.

The second work, which may be considered as an immediate model for Chaucer, is the *Decameron* by Giovanni Boccaccio. Chaucer travelled to Italy and may have met Boccaccio; it is certainly true that he knew the Italian poet's work and was probably trying to create an equivalent masterpiece in English. The framework of the *Decameron* is similar to that of *The Canterbury Tales*, in that 10 narrators are given the task of telling 10 stories each over the course of 10 days, making a neat 100 stories in all. Chaucer's scheme has 30 narrators telling 4 stories each, making a more substantial total of 120 tales. The fact that this scheme came nowhere near completion, and that Chaucer probably reduced the plan to a single tale for each teller, does not reduce the significance of the comparison.

Chaucer's friend John Gower also produced a story collection, suggesting the popularity of such works in the fourteenth century. Gower's *Confessio Amantis* ('Confession of the Lover') is a moral work commenting on the **seven deadly sins**, the same theme as the sermon in 'The Parson's Tale'. Gower also used some of the same stories as Chaucer, notably the tale of Florent (also told by the Wife of Bath) and the tale of Constance ('The Man of Law's Tale').

The Canterbury Tales as a story collection

The difference between Chaucer's work and these other story collections is the dynamic link between the tellers and the tales. The *Gesta Romanorum* has no narrator

at all; it is merely a collection of separate tales. Although there are ten separate narrators in the *Decameron*, there is no great significance in who tells which tale. In Chaucer's work, the match of tale and teller is frequently a crucial part of the overall meaning. The Knight, the most courtly figure on the pilgrimage, tells a suitably courtly tale. The Miller, the most vulgar of the pilgrims, tells the coarsest story. In the most sophisticated case, the Pardoner, who would be a profitable subject for modern psychoanalysis, introduces his tale by explaining the hypocritical success of his own sales techniques, and then proceeds to attempt to dupe his auditors in exactly the same way. As part of this he tells a devastatingly effective tale of greed and justice, which is integrally linked to both his personality and his practices.

The Canterbury Tales is remarkable because it contains examples of all the kinds of story popular in the medieval period — courtly tales, sermons, saints' lives, fabliaux, animal fables — and different verse forms, as well as two tales in prose. This makes *The Canterbury Tales* one of the most diverse of all story collections, and the **narrative** device of the pilgrimage plays an important part in giving this mix cohesion.

It can be difficult to appreciate the significance of Chaucer's overall scheme, both because of the unfinished nature of *The Canterbury Tales*, and because A-level students are usually restricted to studying a tale in isolation. It is strongly recommended that you acquaint yourself with *The Canterbury Tales* as a whole, perhaps by reading the complete work in Modern English.

Chaucer's audience and purpose

Audience

Chaucer was a courtly writer, composing his works for a courtly and sophisticated audience. In earlier eras, almost all culture would have been oral and communal, with storytellers and poets reciting their works to diverse groups of listeners. The only 'books' were manuscripts that were copied by hand onto parchment made from animal skins, and would have been rare and valuable. Almost all manuscripts were of religious texts, and it was not until the later Middle Ages that manuscripts of secular works like Chaucer's became available (more than 80 copies of *The Canterbury Tales* survive). By Chaucer's time, there were sufficient numbers of educated people and manuscript copies to enable private reading parties where one person, for example a lady of the court, would read stories to small groups of friends. An individual might even read stories alone, but that would necessitate the availability of a manuscript, and leisure to peruse it.

Despite these developments, the main mode of communication was still the public performance. It is helpful to think of Chaucer's original audience listening

to *The Canterbury Tales* rather than reading them. No doubt Chaucer read his work to groups at court on frequent occasions, and his audience was mixed, with members of different social groups and classes present. In this sense, Chaucer's situation would have been similar to that of Shakespeare, who had to construct dramas that would appeal to the widest possible taste and intellect. *The Canterbury Tales* includes plenty of entertaining moments to elicit the most superficial of responses, yet also contains subtle and sophisticated elements.

Another development was that Chaucer was identified by name as an author and was popular in his own lifetime. Before this, almost all art was anonymous — the work of art mattered, not its creator.

Purpose

This consideration of Chaucer's audience leads to the vexed question of Chaucer's intentions in composing *The Canterbury Tales*, a subject to which there is no definitive answer.

Irony

Irony is the dominant tone throughout *The Canterbury Tales*, and this makes Chaucer's work elusive and his purpose difficult to define. Irony always depends on personal interpretation, but not all interpretations are equally justifiable or defensible, so be sure that yours are based on wide and careful reading.

'The Miller's Prologue and Tale' is deliberately less subtle than most, but it is still worth being attentive to the depth of Chaucer's craft. Consider lines 347–48 of 'The Merchant's Tale':

> Ye, blessed be alwey a lewed man
> That noght but oonly his bileve kan!

In a simple sense, this seems to indicate John's reliance on simple belief, and distrust of education and sophistication. But ironies abound. John does not rely only on his belief, his trust in the Christian creed. He rapidly falls prey to Nicholas's apparent learning, believing every word of the absurd tale which Nicholas concocts. In the process he fails to recall the basic Christian teaching that God will never send a second flood. The tale as a whole is designed to show the folly of being 'lewed', for John is outwitted at every turn. However, this in itself is deeply ironic, because the tale is supposedly told by the Miller, himself described a 'lewed' by the Reeve in 'The Miller's Prologue' (line 37). Chaucer has an ignorant man make fun of an ignorant man. This is the greater irony of the lines, because it reminds us that we are in fact listening to a subtle literary creation by a master artist, who would never favour ignorance over knowledge. A good A-Level student will be able to handle the sophisticated response required, a fact which Chaucer would have applauded.

Possible interpretations

Modern readers must make up their own minds as to what they are going to gain from studying Chaucer, and this is often a reflection of what they bring to their studies. You will probably find evidence for all the approaches suggested below, but it is up to you to decide what Chaucer has to offer, and how he is to be interpreted in the twenty-first century.

Entertainment

Chaucer's tales are entertaining, and some readers wish to look no further than that. John Carrington, in *Our Greatest Writers and their Major Works* (How To Books, 2003), says simply: 'Chaucer has no over-arching moral or philosophical intention', and that he 'is driven by a curiosity and sympathy for life that excludes the judgemental'.

Social comment

Many readers find some degree of comment on the behaviour and manners of medieval society. This could be anything from wry observation to serious **satire**, e.g. a satire on the three estates class system or a developed thesis on the nature of marriage.

Moral teaching

Chaucer himself, in the 'Retraction' included at the end of *The Canterbury Tales*, quotes from St Paul's comment in the New Testament that all literature contains a moral lesson.

Devotional literature

As a development of the previous point, readers may consider the Christian framework of *The Canterbury Tales* and the idea that it preaches specifically Christian doctrines. The vast majority of medieval literature is religious in this sense, e.g. the mystery plays, such as the Coventry and York cycles, are based on Bible stories. *The Canterbury Tales* finishes with 'The Parson's Tale', a sermon about the **seven deadly sins**, encouraging many to interpret them as having a Christian message about behaviour and morality.

Allegory

Medieval people were familiar with allegory, in which a surface narrative contains one or more further parallel layers of meaning. Such ideas were familiar from Christ's parables in the Bible, and the whole Bible was interpreted allegorically in the Middle Ages. It is possible to see Chaucer as an allegorist in whole or part; Robert P. Miller, writing in the *Companion to Chaucer Studies* (Oxford University Press, 1968), comments: 'Each pilgrim tells his tale from his own point of view, but this point of view is finally to be measured in the perspective afforded by the allegorical system.'

The framework of *The Canterbury Tales*

'The General Prologue' introduces *The Canterbury Tales* and establishes the framework that will underpin the diverse collection of tales that follow. It is worth considering the *Tales* as a whole to see what Chaucer was trying to achieve. It is well known that Chaucer left the work unfinished when he died in 1400, and it has traditionally been assumed that we have only a fragmentary part of what he would eventually have written.

The tales and their tellers

Chaucer's original plan, as revealed in 'The General Prologue', allowed for 30 pilgrims telling 4 tales each, making a total of 120 tales in all. However, only 24 tales exist, 4 of which are unfinished, and although as the *Tales* stand nearly every pilgrim tells a tale, they only tell 1 each.

It is clear that Chaucer drastically modified his original plan, although he never altered 'The General Prologue' to confirm this. There is an excellent reason for his changes. In Chaucer's hands, the tales and tellers are matched with great care, so that one illuminates the other. This is conspicuously true of characters such as the Wife of Bath and the Pardoner. To give these characters more than one tale would gain nothing, and would in fact weaken the effectiveness of the link between tale and teller. In this way Chaucer breaks out of the traditional mould of story collections, in which the character of the narrator is largely unimportant; *The Thousand and One Nights*, for example, has a single narrator for all of its diverse stories.

The significance of the connection between the pilgrims and their tales is emphasised by the only character to tell two tales: Chaucer himself. He starts off with the tale of 'Sir Thopas', but this is told so feebly that the Host (hardly the most astute of critics) interrupts him and tells him to stop. Chaucer thereby achieves the double effect of satirising the weak and formulaic narrative verse of his own time, and creating a joke against himself. His revenge is to let the pilgrim Chaucer follow up with 'a lytel thing in prose', the extended and deeply moral 'Tale of Melibee'. Given that the only other prose piece in *The Canterbury Tales* is 'The Parson's Tale', a meditation on penance, the author may well intend that the pilgrim Chaucer's tale be regarded as one of the most important pieces in the collection, although it is not at all to modern taste.

It is therefore likely that *The Canterbury Tales* is much nearer to completion than a consideration of Chaucer's original plan suggests. However, there are certain anomalies that Chaucer would have needed to address:

- The Yeoman, the Ploughman and the Five Guildsmen lack tales. The absence of 'The Ploughman's Tale' is a particular loss, given the iconic status of ploughmen, as established by Chaucer's contemporary William Langland in *Piers Plowman*.

- 'The Cook's Tale' and 'The Squire's Tale' are unfinished and simply break off part way through; the Knight interrupts the Monk, and the Host halts the doggerel tale of 'Sir Thopas'.
- There are occasional discrepancies in the assignation of tales to tellers; e.g. 'The Shipman's Tale' is clearly intended to have a female narrator.
- In several cases there is no significant connection between tale and teller, although this may be intentional.
- Some of the tales do not have links between them, and the final sequence of the tales is not established.

Taken as a whole, however, it is possible to discern a powerful and unified work that closely reflects Chaucer's final intentions.

The table below shows the order in which the pilgrims are introduced in 'The General Prologue' and the length of their tales.

Character	Lines in 'The General Prologue'	Number of lines	Tale	Number of lines in tale	Order in Robinson's edition
1 Knight	43–78	36	'The Knight's Tale'	2,250	1
2 Squire	79–100	22	'The Squire's Tale'	664	11 (unfinished)
3 Yeoman	101–17	17	–	–	–
4 Prioress	118–62	45	'The Prioress's Tale'	203	16
5 Second Nun	163–64	$1\frac{1}{2}$	'The Second Nun's Tale'	434	21
6–8 Three Priests	164	$\frac{1}{2}$	'The Nun's Priest's Tale'	626	20
9 Monk	165–207	43	'The Monk's Tale'	776	19 (unfinished)
10 Friar	208–69	62	'The Friar's Tale'	364	7
11 Merchant	270–84	15	'The Merchant's Tale'	1,174	10
12 Clerk	285–308	24	'The Clerk's Tale'	1,120	9
13 Man of Law	309–30	22	'The Man of Law's Tale'	1,028	5
14 Franklin	331–60	30	'The Franklin's Tale'	896	12
15–19 Five Guildsmen	361–78	18	–	–	–
20 Cook	379–87	9	'The Cook's Tale'	58	4 (unfinished)
21 Shipman	388–410	23	'The Shipman's Tale'	434	15
22 Doctor of Physic	411–44	34	'The Physician's Tale'	286	13
23 Wife of Bath	445–76	32	'The Wife of Bath's Tale'	408	6
24 Parson	477–528	52	'The Parson's Tale'	1.005 (prose)	24
25 Ploughman	529–41	13	–	–	–
26 Miller	542–66	25	'The Miller's Tale'	668	2
27 Manciple	567–86	20	'The Manciple's Tale'	258	23

Character	Lines in 'The General Prologue'	Number of lines	Tale	Number of lines in tale	Order in Robinson's edition
28 Reeve	587–622	36	'The Reeve's Tale'	403	3
29 Summoner	623–68	46	'The Summoner's Tale'	586	8
30 Pardoner	669–714	46	'The Pardoner's Tale'	506	14
31 Chaucer	–	–	'Sir Thopas'	207	17 (unfinished)
			'The Tale of Melibee'	922 (prose)	18
32 Canon	–	–	–	–	–
33 Canon's Yeoman	–	–	'The Canon's Yeoman's Tale'	762	22

The multiple narrator in *The Canterbury Tales*

In a conventional novel, the action is mediated to the reader by a narrator:

Narrator
⬇
Audience

In *The Canterbury Tales*, Chaucer introduces further **narrative** levels that offer the opportunity for much greater subtlety. First, Chaucer the author introduces himself as a character or persona within the text, so that the situation is as follows:

Chaucer the author
⬇
Chaucer the pilgrim
⬇
Audience

This means that when you come across a remark in 'The General Prologue' like 'And I seyde his opinion was good', it is ostensibly made by Chaucer the pilgrim. The reader must decide how far it may also be Chaucer the author's view.

When it comes to the tales themselves, a further layer of complexity is added because each tale is told by one of the pilgrims and reported by Chaucer the pilgrim. The narrative reaches its audience at three removes from its author:

Chaucer the author
⬇
Chaucer the pilgrim
⬇
Pilgrim narrator
⬇
Audience

Finally, when a character within one of the tales speaks a fifth narrative layer is added:

Chaucer the author

⬇

Chaucer the pilgrim

⬇

Pilgrim narrator

⬇

Character

⬇

Audience

The attentive reader must decide how far each of the narrating figures is in accord with what is being said. The example already considered on p. 27 is pertinent here:

> Ye, blessed be alwey a lewed man
> That noght but oonly his bileve kan! (lines 347–48)

John is sincere in what he says, but does the Miller as narrator agree, or is he mocking him? Chaucer the pilgrim would probably accept that honest belief is better than suspect intellectualising, but Chaucer the author certainly asks his audience to balance the merits of unthinking belief against learned knowledge. It is in this layered interpretation of Chaucer's writing that critical debate takes place, and every student should have his/her own opinion.

Chaucer the pilgrim as narrator

The subtlety in Chaucer's craft arises from the device of the pilgrim narrator. This persona is portrayed as a sociable but rather diffident character. When the time comes for him to tell his own tale the Host thinks he looks 'elvyssh' (otherworldly) and shy: 'For evere upon the ground I se thee stare' ('Prologue to Sir Thopas', line 697). Chaucer the pilgrim begins to tell a poor story ('Sir Thopas'), but once interrupted by the Host he launches into a long, moral, prose narrative ('The Tale of Melibee'), which shows his erudition and seriousness. In 'The General Prologue', Chaucer the pilgrim frequently appears to be naive, most famously when he agrees with the Monk's low opinion of his own vows ('And I seyde his opinion was good', line 183). Often this encourages the other pilgrims to make further indiscreet confessions about their behaviour, such as the Monk revealing his obsession with hunting and riding. When Chaucer the pilgrim does wish to comment directly on a character, he can do so, as in the case of the Summoner: 'But wel I woot he lied right in dede' (line 661).

Chaucer's verse

The **metre** that Chaucer adopted for most of *The Canterbury Tales* became the standard one used in English poetry for the next 500 years, and in this

sense at least he should be familiar to the modern reader. He writes in **iambic pentameter**, the metre used by Shakespeare, Milton, Keats and all of the great poets prior to the twentieth century. The lines are arranged into pairs called **heroic couplets**.

'Iambic' refers to the rhythm of the verse: a repeated pattern of two syllables, with the first syllable being unstressed and the second syllable being stressed, as in words like 'remind' and 'believe'. An iamb is one of these two-syllable, unstressed/stressed patterns. Each pair of syllables is called a foot. 'Pentameter' (literally five measures or 'feet') means that five feet are joined together to make a ten-syllable (decasyllabic) regular line: da dum da dum da dum da dum da dum. The conventional mark for a stressed syllable is /, and the mark for an unstressed syllable is ~. A couplet of iambic pentameter therefore goes like this:

> ~ / ~ / ~ / ~ / ~ /
> But of hir song, it was as loude and yerne,

> ~ / ~ / ~ / ~ / ~ /
> As any swalwe sittinge on a berne.   ('The Miller's Tale', lines 149–50)

The reason that this became the staple metre of English poetry is because iambic rhythm is closest to natural speech — whenever you speak a sentence, it contains more iambs than any other rhythm.

Chaucer shows astonishing assurance and versatility in handling the iambic form. He can use it for stately formal descriptions:

> His rode was reed, his eyen greye as goos.
> With Poules window corven on his shoos,
> In hoses rede he wente fetisly.   (ibid., lines 209–11)

He can use it for fast-paced action:

> He sit him up withouten wordes mo,
> And with his ax he smoot the corde atwo,
> And doun gooth al;   (ibid., lines 711–13)

He uses it for **rhetorical** declamation by the narrator:

> Lo, which a greet thing is affeccioun!   (ibid., line 503)

But most frequently and most effectively he uses it to represent speech:

> And thus they been accorded and ysworn
> To waite a time as I have told biforn.   (ibid., lines 193–94)

> 'What! Nicholay! what, how! what, looke adoun!
> Awak, and thenk on Cristes passioun!'   (ibid., lines 369–70)

In his earlier work, Chaucer frequently used an octosyllabic (eight-syllable) line, which was common at the time; the iambic pentameter marks his maturity as a poet.

Chaucer's language

There is no doubt that the Middle English of *The Canterbury Tales* comes between the modern reader and an easy appreciation of the work. However, after a little practice most of the difficulties presented by the language drop away. Note that the vocabulary can present problems, because some words look familiar or obvious, and aren't. For example, the word 'wood' can mean wood but, in a different context, means mad, as in the description of the carpenter at the end of 'The Miller's Tale' (line 738). The solution is to keep a careful eye on the notes and glossary of your edition.

Reading aloud

The easiest way to start to understand Chaucer's language is to read it aloud, or to listen to it being read. Chaucer intended his verse to be spoken, and it makes more sense when it is. Remember the following:

- Most letters are pronounced, so that 'knight' sounds like 'cnicht' and 'mighte' like 'micht'.
- The final 'e' on words like 'herbes' ('herb-es') is normally pronounced, unless it is followed by another vowel.
- Some vowels have different sound values, but don't worry about this initially.
- Words imported from French would still sound French, so 'rage' would be 'rage' and 'mariage' would be 'mar-ee-arge'.

With these few simple adjustments, aim to read the verse as if it were ordinary conversation. Try to ignore the rhythm and rhyme — they'll take care of themselves. Your edition should have further detail on aspects of pronunciation, but the primary objective is to get a sense of the flow of the language.

Modernisations

Another good way of gaining confidence in reading the language is to create a Modern English version of each line. This can be done aloud in class, or you can jot down a literal version as you go along, for example:

Whilom ther was dwellinge at Oxenford
Once there was living in Oxford
A riche gnof, that gestes heeld to bord,
A rich knave who took in lodgers

It isn't long before Chaucer's English becomes almost as straightforward as Shakespeare's. You never quite lose your caution in looking at it (as you shouldn't with Shakespeare), but you do become more comfortable working with it.

It may be a good idea to obtain a modern version of 'The Miller's Prologue and Tale', and even of the whole of *The Canterbury Tales*. This will allow you to check your own rendering of each line, so that you are confident that you have the correct basic meaning.

The Miller in 'The General Prologue'

This is how the Miller is introduced in 'The General Prologue' (lines 547–68). The modernised English version (in italics) is entirely literal, and is given to help clarify the meaning of the passage.

> The MILLERE was a stout carl for the nones;
> *The Miller was a well-built fellow,*
> Ful big he was of brawn, and eek of bones.
> *With big muscles and big bones too.*
> That proved wel, for over al ther he cam,
> *That was useful, because wherever he went*
> 550 At wrastlinge he wolde have alwey the ram.
> *He would always win the prize at wrestling.*
> He was short-sholdred, brood, a thikke knarre;
> *He was squat and broad, a thickset knave;*
> There was no dore that he nolde heve of harre,
> *There was no door that he couldn't heave off its hinges*
> Or breke it at a renning with his heed.
> *Or break by running at it with his head.*
> His berd as any sowe or fox was reed,
> *His beard was as red as a pig or a fox,*
> 555 And therto brood, as though it were a spade.
> *And as wide as a spade.*
> Upon the cop right of his nose he hade
> *Right on the tip of his nose*
> A werte, and theron stood a toft of heris,
> *There was a wart, with a tuft of hairs on it,*
> Reed as the brustles of a sowis eris;
> *Red as the bristles in a sow's ears;*

His nosethirles blake were and wide.
His nostrils were wide and black.

560 A swerd and bokeler bar he by his side.
He carried a sword and shield at his side.

His mouth as greet was as a greet forneys.
His mouth was like a great furnace.

He was a janglere and a goliardeys,
He was a chatterer and a jester,

And that was moost of sinne and harlotries.
And that was mostly of sin and misdeeds.

Wel koude he stelen corn and tollen thries;
He knew how to steal corn and charge three times the proper price;

565 And yet he hadde a thombe of gold, pardee.
And indeed he had a thumb of gold.

A whit cote and a blew hood wered he.
He wore a white coat and a blue hood.

A baggepipe wel koude he blowe and sowne,
He was good at playing the bagpipes,

And therwithal he broghte us out of towne.
And with that accompaniment he led us out of the city

The Miller's portrait is extremely unsubtle, as befits the nature of the character being described. Nevertheless, there are details in it which require some close observation if their full significance is to be appreciated.

A sinful oaf

The Miller's physical description ('The General Prologue', lines 552–53) is of a burly, thickset and strong man, a brainless oaf of the type still **caricatured** today:

Ther was no dore that he nolde heve of harre,
Or breke it at a renning with his heed.

He is also unscrupulous, and Chaucer states this directly too:

Wel koude he stelen corn and tollen thries;
And yet he hadde a thombe of gold, pardee. (lines 564–65)

The latter line is a conventional jibe about millers, referring to the colour of their thumbs from handling the corn, and their traditional dishonesty and profiteering.

The portrait is given an extra dimension by the details of the Miller's physical description. His mouth, 'as greet…as a greet forneys' (line 561), spews forth 'sinne and harlotries' (line 563), and is reminiscent of medieval illustrations of the mouth of Hell. This allusion is furthered by his choice of instrument, 'a baggepipe wel koude he blowe and sowne' (line 567); bagpipes were traditionally played by the

devil, and the Miller's portrait deepens from that of a mere rogue to that of a corrupt and condemned sinner. It was a commonplace of medieval thinking that a person's physical appearance was a direct manifestation of his/her inner being: a good person would be beautiful (and vice versa), whereas a character as physically gross as the Miller would clearly be a sinful man.

Leading the pilgrims

It is a typically mischievous touch of Chaucer's to make the Miller the leader of the pilgrimage ('And therwithal he broghte us out of towne' (line 568)) and to ensure that he tells an early tale of unparalleled depravity. Although there are other pilgrims who are more corrupt than the Miller, notably the Summoner and the Pardoner, there are none so obviously lacking in moral qualities.

Making the Miller leader of the band of pilgrims can be seen as a jest by Chaucer on a larger scale; he perhaps poses the question: if the devil leads them, how many of the pilgrims have the moral integrity to resist his temptations? That question underlies the whole of *The Canterbury Tales*, just as it underlay the life of every medieval person.

Making sense of the story

Summary

John, a rich old Oxford carpenter, has married the young and pretty Alison. His lodger, a poor scholar named Nicholas, woos Alison and gains her love. She is also fancied by a young priest's assistant called Absolon, who woos her incessantly and in vain.

Nicholas and Alison hatch a plan to trick the carpenter, so that they can spend the night together. Nicholas uses his knowledge of astrology to persuade John that there is going to be a second Flood. He fools John into making preparations for this by placing three tubs in the roof, into which they all climb that night. John conveniently falls asleep, and Nicholas and Alison go down and spend the night in bed together.

At dawn, Absolon arrives and begs a kiss from Alison. She responds by putting her bottom out of the window, and when he kisses this he is revolted and wants revenge. He goes and gets a hot coulter or ploughblade from a smithy, then returns to the house. He asks for another kiss, but this time Nicholas presents his posterior. Absolon smites it with the coulter; Nicholas's cries awaken the carpenter who, thinking the Flood has begun, cuts the tethers of his tub and crashes to the floor, breaking his arm. Nicholas and Alison persuade the neighbours that the carpenter's predicament has been caused by his own fantasies.

John's lodger

John probably keeps lodgers to increase his social status rather than because he needs the money; he is after all a 'riche gnof' (line 80). Nicholas is obviously a student at Oxford University, which was founded in the twelfth century.

Alison's readiness to deceive her husband

This deception is at the core of the tale. Although there is no direct comment on Alison's motivation, it seems that both she and Nicholas are young and attractive, whereas her husband is the traditional **stereotype** of a jealous old man: 'For she was wilde and yong, and he was old' (line 117).

Alison's rejection of Absolon

There are two reasons for Alison's rejection of Absolon's advances. First, she already has a lover in Nicholas (lines 277–90). Second, because she is 'wilde' (line 117) she prefers Nicholas's direct and crude approach to Absolon's ridiculous courting, which is a caricature of **courtly love** and therefore unlikely to make an impression on a carpenter's wife. In her eyes, Absolon is effeminate and self-obsessed.

The way Nicholas fools John

The plan to deceive John is surprisingly elaborate, which adds to its comedic effect. Nicholas hides in his room, as if he were ill, in order to provoke John's curiosity and concern. He is discovered behaving like a lunatic (lines 336–37), making a great impression on John, even if the latter condemns Nicholas's studies. It is then easy for Nicholas to make John believe that he has been able to use astrology to foresee the future and that what he says is God's own commandment, which parallels God's instructions to Noah when the original Flood occurred. To understand why John would accept Nicholas's authority, you should consider the medieval understanding of the way the universe operated, and the concomitant belief in astrology. Events on Earth were believed to be affected by the movements of the planets, and Nicholas is an expert on the subject. The simple-minded carpenter is taken in by the hocus-pocus.

Nicholas's story of the flood

Nicholas is specific in his description, making his 'vision' more credible, at least to the gullible John. He says that the flood will arrive the next evening (Monday) at about 9 p.m. ('at quarter night' (line 408)), leaving Nicholas and Alison a full night of lovemaking. The flood will cover the whole world 'in lasse than an hour' (line 411), and all mankind will be drowned, as in the original Flood (line 413). He offers to save John, Alison and himself, although John will do the actual work by preparing three tubs or troughs, provisioned like life rafts, and hanging them in

the roof of the house. John's servants cannot be saved, although Nicholas does not waste time explaining why not, instead saying that it is God's secret (lines 447–50). The flood will only last, he says, until 9 the next morning, and will then vanish (lines 445–46). During the night it is necessary for the three of them to sit in their separate tubs, not speaking nor looking at each other, so that there is no sin between them (lines 481–82). When the flood occurs they will cut the ropes on their tubs and break a hole in the roof, through which they will float on the water until the flood subsides. Nicholas even creates a picture for John of them floating like ducks and calling out to each other (lines 465–72). As a final incentive to obey him exactly, Nicholas states that after the flood they will be rulers of the world, as Noah and his sons were (lines 473–74).

John's reaction to Nicholas's story

John accepts Nicholas's story without question or reservation, believing it to be God's will. His only concern is for Alison, 'his hony deere' (line 509); he shows no concern for his servants or for the rest of mankind, or even for himself. He does exactly what Nicholas has demanded of him in every respect, and then conveniently falls asleep as soon as he has climbed into his tub on Monday evening (lines 535–37). By this means, Chaucer carefully avoids making the audience feel sympathy for John.

Absolon's visit to the house

Absolon decides to visit the house at cock-crow (lines 567 and 579), which is an hour or so before dawn (an important point, as everything happens in pitch darkness). At Alison's window he coughs and calls out; when she tells him to go away he asks her for a kiss. As a way of getting rid of him she agrees, but puts her backside out of the window. He kisses it and is baffled because it is hairy (lines 628–31). When he realises what has happened Absolon is disgusted, and tries to clean his mouth (lines 639–40); his amorous obsession is cured (lines 646–49).

Desiring revenge, he goes to a smithy, where Gervase the smith is already at work, and acquires a coulter — the sharp end of a ploughshare. He returns to the window and coughs as he did before. Nicholas, having 'risen for to pisse' (line 690), decides to further the joke by getting Absolon to kiss his backside; he farts in Absolon's face, whereon Absolon strikes him with the coulter so that the skin is burnt 'an hande-brede aboute' (line 703). Nicholas's cries for 'water! water!' (line 707) wake John, who thinks that the flood has started and cuts the ropes of his tub, crashing to the floor and breaking his arm (lines 708–15).

The end of the tale

Alison and Nicholas raise a commotion (lines 716–17) that rouses the neighbours, who come in to stare at the scene. John's protestations are overridden by the lovers'

insistence that he is mad (lines 723–25) and did everything 'thurgh fantasie' (line 727) in fear of Noah's Flood. The whole town comes to believe that he is mad, and laughs at him. If the audience expected a clear moral ending, the Miller does not offer one.

Characters

John

The carpenter is rich, old and stupid, a jealous man who is obsessed with his young wife. His primary characteristic is his gullibility, which permits both the events and the comedy of the tale to take place.

The word 'sely' is used five times about John. 'Sely' is one of the most fascinating words in the English language. It originally meant 'holy' ('selig' in Old English), and gradually shifted meaning through 'pure', 'innocent', 'simple' and 'foolish', until it arrived in modern English as the word 'silly'. In Chaucer's Middle English its main area of meaning was 'naive', and it points to John's lack of intelligence, wit or perceptiveness.

Nicholas

The scholar is poor, young and clever. Unlike the other characters, he receives no extended description at the beginning of the tale, but is identified primarily through his obsession with astrology, which will be the means by which he dupes the carpenter.

The word 'hende' is used no less than ten times about Nicholas. 'Hende' is difficult to define, and no single interpretation will do. Its main area of meaning was 'courteous', 'polite' and 'gentle', and it was usually employed in a complimentary sense. Its repeated use as an **epithet** for Nicholas can hardly go unremarked; no other character in Chaucer receives such a leitmotif. His behaviour is anything but courteous, so it is probable that we are meant to see 'hende' as indicating the outward behaviour of the man, the plausible and smooth-talking scholar who can persuade John into any belief he chooses, and who convinces the neighbours at the end of the tale that the carpenter has been hallucinating. Underneath is a devious schemer.

The contrast between John and Nicholas

There is a strong contrast between the two characters, which is emphasised at every point in the tale. They are respectively described as 'riche' (line 80) and 'poure' (line 82). Where John is 'sely', Nicholas is 'sleigh and ful privee' (line 93) and 'subtil and ful queynte' (line 167). Where John is just a carpenter (like the Reeve, whom

the Miller wished to insult), Nicholas is an educated man and a musician — a classic confrontation between a working man and an intellectual. John shelters behind his lack of learning ('Ye, blessed be alwey a lewed man' (line 347)), and Nicholas uses precisely this quality to bamboozle him into believing nonsense about a one-night flood. The choice of flood as the method of trickery is particularly appropriate, as this is the one disaster that God promised never to send on mankind again; the fact that John accepts Nicholas's story so readily demonstrates the depths of his simplicity.

Alison

Alison is 18 years old, pretty and 'wilde' (line 117). The long description of her at the beginning of the tale follows conventional medieval ideas about beauty, as does the way she falls for Nicholas. She pretends to refuse him, but only to the extent of claiming that she will protest if he persists; she does not in fact cry 'out, harrow' and 'allas' (line 178), as she threatens to do. Three lines later she offers him her love, and her only concern thereafter is how they can deceive her husband.

Much of the description of Alison is in the form of a blazon, a device in medieval poetry whereby a woman's body is described and celebrated in detail. It uses conventional phrases and attributes: she is delicate and slender, she has black hair and a shining complexion, she sings like a bird. However, Chaucer — or the Miller — lays particular stress on her physicality, using animal **imagery** to evoke her charms and describing her in rousing terms as a 'wenche' (line 146), a 'primerole' and a 'piggesnie' (line 160). He focuses on her mouth, 'sweete as bragot or the meeth' (line 153), and her limbs, with 'shoes laced on hir legges hye' (line 159), to emphasise her sensuality.

This description is wholly in line with her behaviour throughout the tale, and overall there is no sense of her being a developed individual; she is a straightforward representation of the unfaithful young wife. She gives in to Nicholas with only token resistance, she lies to her husband ('I am thy trewe, verray wedded wyf', (line 501)), and her treatment of Absolon is crude in every sense. She is a typically 'low' character in accordance with the **fabliau genre** of the tale (see p. 47).

Absolon

This young parish priest is obsessed with his own appearance and believes himself attractive to women; he is fastidious in his habits and manner. Like Alison, he is introduced with an extended description (lines 203–30), the picture of an effete and self-obsessed man, with the sole individual — and absurd — characteristic of being 'somdeel squaymous/Of fartyng' (lines 229–30).

Even if some elements of Absolon's portrait are common in medieval images, like his red complexion and grey eyes, the most striking characteristic is his narcissism. He wears a white surplice over red leggings; his hair and shoes are

carefully described, as is his habit of playing the giterne (a guitar-like instrument) and touring the taverns in the hope of attracting one of the barmaids. The final **couplet** of his description (lines 229–30) is a notably individual touch, in keeping with the **tone** of the tale, which both subverts his description by introducing the coarse topic of farting, and prepares the ground for his final humiliation by Nicholas.

Absolon's wooing of Alison

Absolon's mode of wooing is absurd. The way he ogles all the women in church is laughably irreligious, and the fact that he will not accept their church donations, which he believes are for him, because of his 'love-longinge' (line 241) makes him a figure of ridicule. This comic impression is reinforced in the way he attempts to woo Alison, singing outside her window so that he wakes her husband, and showering her with gifts and attentions that make him seem obsessive — the prototype of the modern stalker.

These ludicrous and obsessive qualities define Absolon's character, and also explain his behaviour in the latter part of the tale. When he discovers that Alison's husband is apparently absent, he takes the opportunity to go to her window, seemingly oblivious of the likely presence of Nicholas, and addresses her in soppy language that would probably receive the most contemptuous of replies even if she were not in bed with her lover at the time. He calls her 'hony-comb', 'faire brid', 'sweete cinamome' and 'lemman myn' (lines 590–92), which would be nauseating enough if they were the intimacies of lovers, and are ridiculous coming from a wooer. The same is true of his preparations for this meeting, where he chews 'greyn and licoris' (line 582) to sweeten his breath, 'for therby wende he to ben gracious' (line 585). The coarse nature of his disillusionment, kissing Alison's hairy backside, is the shock he needs to cure him of his delusions, and results in revulsion so extravagant that it matches his former infatuation, as he scrubs his lips 'With dust, with sond, with straw, with clooth, with chippes' (line 640). The crude nature of his revenge, with a hot coulter or ploughblade intended for Alison, is also in line with his egregious behaviour. In every way Absolon is a ridiculous figure, and there is no prospect of the audience sympathising with him at any stage. You should consider how far the **characterisation** of Absolon is part of a satire of courtly love (see below).

Themes

Marriage

'The Miller's Tale' presents a marriage of opposites. John is old, Alison is young; he is stupid, she is cunning. The key passage is lines 113–24, which directly states

their discrepancies, to the point that the carpenter 'demed himself been lik a cokewold' (line 118), even before anything takes place.

The comic unsuitability of the match between John and Alison is a primary aspect of the tale for both the Miller and Chaucer. The Miller clearly wishes to satirise marriage, showing the folly of an old man thinking that he can control a young wife, and the immorality of young women who cannot be trusted.

As far as Chaucer is concerned, the inclusion of this tale establishes the subject of marriage and true relationships, which occupies him for much of *The Canterbury Tales*. He takes an early opportunity to present an example of a comically bad marriage, a theme he will return to several times, notably in 'The Wife of Bath's Prologue and Tale' and 'The Merchant's Tale'.

Carpenters

The Miller has a further purpose in making a particular point about the stupidity of carpenters, because he hates the Reeve, who trained as a carpenter in his youth. The latter is stung into telling a savage tale about millers as a riposte. The antagonism between the Miller and the Reeve, set up in 'The General Prologue' and developed in 'The Miller's Prologue', creates a natural link to the next tale (the Reeve's), and makes *The Canterbury Tales* seem a more naturalistic and organic work.

Courtly love

The tale has been seen specifically as a satire of courtly love. This literary invention of the Middle Ages was a set of rules governing the behaviour of aristocratic lovers. The lady would be idealised, and idolised, by her noble lover, who would devote himself wholly to her service and perform numerous tasks in order to demonstrate his faith and his love; he would remain true even if ignored or rejected by the object of his devotion.

'The Knight's Tale', the first of *The Canterbury Tales* and the one that precedes 'The Miller's Tale', presents courtly love in this way. Two noble cousins, Palamon and Arcite, fall in love with the same woman, Emily, who is unaware of their existence. They endure many trials over a period of years before eventually jousting against one another for the right to marry her. Palamon is defeated, but Arcite is thrown from his horse and dies, so it is Palamon who is finally successful.

There is an obvious contrast between the courtly nature of Absolon's wooing, with his go-betweens and presents and songs, and Nicholas's direct approach: 'And prively he caughte hire by the queynte' (line 168). Absolon's behaviour is absurd at every point, and the irony lies in the inappropriateness of following courtly love conventions (lines 263–76) when wooing the earthy wife of a carpenter.

The Miller may merely be making fun of courtly behaviour, showing Nicholas's method to be more effective, but Chaucer seems to demand that his audience be more thoughtful, and compare the relationships here with the truly courtly ones of

'The Knight's Tale', which immediately precedes the Miller's. He appears keen to introduce the full range of social behaviour early on in *The Canterbury Tales*, so that his audience's response is framed against a complete moral canvas.

Youth and age

The traditional disparity between the lecherous old man and the flighty young wife is so conventional as to need no introduction to any audience, ancient or modern. There is no subtlety to this scenario, merely the enjoyment of seeing the way the old man is fooled despite all his precautions.

In 'The Miller's Tale', the old husband is made particularly naive and stupid, so that although he is 'jalous' he seems to be unaware of the likely attraction between his wife and his lodger, and although he notices Absolon's singing outside the window he takes no direct steps to dislodge him. This contrasts sharply with the husband in 'The Merchant's Tale', who tries everything to prevent his wife from being unfaithful. The Miller's purpose seems to be to make the old man merely a figure of fun, which will make the Reeve even more annoyed.

'Town and gown'

As well as the contrast between John and Alison, there is the conflict between John and Nicholas, representing the traditional tension between university academics and working people. Nicholas is the intellectual, with his 'bookes grete and smale (line 100), while John is the successful but ignorant tradesman. It is another irony that Chaucer allows the Miller, a man as unintelligent as the carpenter, to tell a tale in which the clever character makes a fool of the stupid one.

The Flood

On a simple level, the theme of the flood adds a further layer of comedy to the tale, and emphasises the carpenter's stupidity. The Flood was the single event that God promised never to repeat, so John's credulous acceptance of Nicholas's invention has increased comic value. It also heightens the comic **climax** of the tale, with the image of John crashing down from the roof amid the chaos where Nicholas is screaming in agony after Absolon's revenge.

It is possible to take a more serious view of the subplot, and this is dealt with in the section on moral vision on pp. 49–51 The original Flood was designed to teach mankind a lesson, and in a minor way the flood in 'The Miller's Tale' does the same thing.

The Church

Chaucer always has a lively sense of the foibles and failings of people in their religious beliefs and practices. In 'The Miller's Tale', there is John's assumption that Nicholas's astrology has driven him mad (lines 340–54), which is then followed by

an equal willingness to believe the power of the same astrology when it warns him of disaster. Absolon's position as a cleric is made absurd by his obsession with women, and Alison in particular (lines 231–37). Chaucer even ironically uses the sound of church bells at the moment when Nicholas and Alison are in bed (lines 545–48), showing that religion, then as now, has difficulty competing with more worldly pleasures.

Humour

'The Miller's Tale' is one of the most humorous of all *The Canterbury Tales*, to the extent that some people would say it has no serious aspect at all. Chaucer makes use of a full range of comic devices, and although there is considerable overlap it is worth trying to define and distinguish various kinds of humour.

Situational humour

The basic situation of the tale is itself comical: a jealous old man is married to a pretty wife, who receives attentions from two young men. The fact that her lover is actually his lodger only emphasises this, as does the fact that both of the wooers are supposedly religious men, one a scholar cleric and the other a lay clerk.

Humorous situational details include the episode of Nicholas's madness, with the servant peering at him through a hole in the door (lines 332–35); Absolon wooing Alison even when she is in bed with her husband (lines 244–61); the elaborateness of Nicholas's plan to evade the flood (lines 455–74); the kiss and its aftermath (lines 622–715).

Satire

The main themes of the tale are all given satirical treatment. There is a ridiculous marriage, the absurd wooing of Absolon and the coarse manner of Nicholas and Alison. The elder man (John) is made a figure of fun, while the younger people all behave badly.

There is a constant tension in the tale between how people ought to behave and how they do behave, the traditional medieval struggle between the temptations of the flesh and the promptings of the soul. This is emphasised by the proximity of the carpenter's house to the church, which should command Absolon's attention but doesn't, and when the church bells are heard even as Nicholas and Alison are in bed together.

Irony

As well as the situational ironies of the story, there is a great deal of verbal irony too, some of which is quite subtle. Alison swearing that she will obey Nicholas (rather

than her husband) 'by Seint Thomas of Kent' (line 183) is inappropriate, given the context in which the tale is being told; it emphasises the depth of her unfaithfulness, a point reinforced by the brazenness of her assertion to John: 'I am thy trewe, verray wedded wyf' (line 501). The parody of courtly love language in Absolon's wooing is similarly comic; the humour derives from the mismatch between the terms used (e.g. lines 590–99) and the low class of the characters involved. In addition, straight-forward ironies, like John's claim that stupidity is a virtue (lines 347–48), are easily identified.

This kind of humour and comic effect is abundant throughout the tale, and you should always be on the alert for what Chaucer is implying beyond the surface meaning.

The ludicrous

Much of the humour of the tale derives from its ludicrous events, despite its super-ficial sense of realism. The idea of the flood lasting a single night, and conveniently vanishing the next morning, is ridiculous, and the fact that John seems to accept this without question only emphasises his gullibility. Many of the details Nicholas adds are outrageous: his claims that the servants cannot be saved, the injunctions to silence and chastity while they are in the tubs, the vision of them hailing each other while floating about, and the preposterous promise that 'thanne shul we be lordes al oure lyf/Of al the world' (lines 473–74). These are progressively silly, as if he is seeing how far he can go before John will start doubting his word, and greatly add to the audience's enjoyment.

The portrayal of Absolon has absurd aspects, particularly the idea that he is fastidious about his own person, and yet seems to have an abhorrence of actual bodies and bodily functions. His squeamishness about farting is mentioned in lines 229–30, but not referred to again until he receives a devastating one ('As greet as it had been a thonder-dent') in line 698 — the most famous fart in English literature.

Bawdy

'The Miller's Tale' is one of the crudest and **bawdiest** of all *The Canterbury Tales*, and is often simply enjoyed as such. The story itself has numerous bawdy elements: Nicholas's wooing of Alison; the lovers enjoying their night of passion while the carpenter sleeps above them; Absolon kissing Alison's backside; Nicholas's fart, and Absolon's revenge.

A modern publisher would hesitate before releasing a novel with language as uncompromising as Chaucer's, but the inclusion of 'queynte' (line 168), 'hole' (line 624), 'ers' (line 626), 'piss' (line 690), 'fart' (line 698), 'toute' (line 704) and 'swived' (line 742) does not trouble Chaucer at all, and presumably his audience

accepted the bawdy aspects of his work with pleasure rather than condemnation. Chaucer certainly excuses himself by assigning all this material to the Miller (who in turn blames it on 'the ale of Southwerk' (line 32)), but the reality is that these coarse elements are part of the fabliau genre (see below), and help to further the contrast and distance that Chaucer establishes between the Miller's story and the Knight's. The result is that by the time the audience has heard the first two of *The Canterbury Tales*, the full range is established from the most sophisticated and courtly tale to the most base and crude. Students might find it interesting to note that even this most coarse of Chaucerian tales is mild by comparison with some of those in *The Thousand and One Nights* (although these are never included in the selections of tales normally presented in translations).

'The Miller's Tale' as a fabliau

In the medieval period, fabliaux were short, comic or satiric tales, realistic rather than idealised, dealing with middle- or lower-class characters rather than the nobility. The setting was normally contemporary, rather than the 'once upon a time' of **romances**, and the language was usually **colloquial** and coarse. They were frequently bawdy or obscene, with characters who tended to flout authority and who were admired more often for their cunning than for their morality. A standard theme was the adultery of a repressed wife, usually with a clever or cunning cleric.

Fabliaux became popular in France in the twelfth and thirteenth centuries, although they were part of the long tradition that lower-class characters were only suitable for comic treatment; lofty themes were reserved for noble characters. This is a tendency that can be observed right back to classical times, and more recently in Shakespeare, where the comic interest in the tragedies is frequently provided by common folk, such as the porter in *Macbeth* or the gravediggers in *Hamlet*.

Chaucer was obviously fond of the fabliau form. Although critics do not agree about a precise definition, the tales of the Miller, the Reeve, the Cook, the Friar, the Summoner, the Merchant and the Shipman are normally labelled fabliaux.

All the standard elements of the fabliau are evident in the 'The Miller's Tale'; in this sense, it is a tale ideally matched to its teller, whose earthy crudeness is in keeping with the matter and the manner of the tale. The subject of the story is typical of the genre: the cuckolding of a foolish husband by a scheming wife, aided by a clever student who outwits the dull-witted carpenter. The whole story is bawdy and obscene, with its emphasis on crude bodily functions — farting, defecation and sex — and the language is appropriately coarse. Such justice as is meted out at the end of the tale is of a primitive and physical kind, and the main transgressor — Alison — isn't punished at all.

However, the allusion to the Flood introduces a religious aspect to the story, albeit an absurdly treated one. The audience is not allowed to detach itself entirely from the underlying seriousness of Chaucer's work, and is therefore invited to place this tale within the context that has already been created by 'The General Prologue' and 'The Knight's Tale'. Chaucer extends the fabliau genre by addressing serious themes, such as marriage and moral behaviour, within a comic framework.

The tale and its teller

The connection between the tale and the teller is an issue throughout *The Canterbury Tales*. Because of the incomplete nature of the project, there is considerable variation in this regard. Some tales are not matched to their narrators at all, for example 'The Nun's Priest's Tale', as the Nun's Priest is left undescribed in 'The General Prologue'. In other cases the match has not been decided, for example in 'The Shipman's Tale' there is evidence that the tale originally had a female narrator. But in some cases the relationship is highly developed. The finest examples are 'The Wife of Bath's Tale' and 'The Pardoner's Tale', in which the tales are perfectly matched to the tellers because each of these characters is given an extended prologue to their own tale — in the Wife of Bath's case, her prologue is twice the length of the tale she tells.

Although the connection is not as developed as this, 'The Miller's Tale' remains one of the most carefully matched. Chaucer has gone to considerable lengths to set up the situation in which the Miller tells his tale, as he has in the choice and nature of the tale the Miller tells.

'The Miller's Prologue'

The impression of the Miller as a coarse and crude man is amply confirmed by his prologue. He interrupts the Host, grossly claims that his tale will be 'noble', and is offensive to the Host and the Reeve. In addition, three new elements are added:

- He is drunk. Although this proclivity is not directly mentioned in 'The General Prologue', it is entirely in keeping with his character. It allows Chaucer to have him break into the sequence of tales begun by the Knight.
- He dislikes the Reeve. The Miller says his tale is about a carpenter, and is rewarded when the Reeve instantly rises to the bait. This hostility between the two characters allows Chaucer to gain maximum comic effect from their tales. The Reeve tells the next tale, and gains his revenge by relating the story of a thieving miller whose wife and daughter both have sex with visiting students.
- Both the Miller ('Robin' (line 21)) and the Reeve ('Osewold' (line 43)) are named. This deepens the sense of realism about the characters and makes their dispute more personal.

The Miller and his tale

The delight in the bawdy tale is entirely appropriate for the Miller, and the way that the carpenter is shown to be especially foolish confirms the Miller's malice against the Reeve. The physicality of the events — the farting, the scalding, the carpenter's broken arm — matches the brutal nature of the Miller revealed in 'The General Prologue'. The willingness to use coarse language is another feature of the blunt and plain-speaking Miller, which he shares with the equally outspoken Wife of Bath.

In terms of subject matter, language and tone, the tale is obviously suited to the Miller; or rather, Chaucer developed the Miller's character to fit the tale he assigned to him. The artistry, sophistication and depth of learning visible in the tale are all Chaucer's; the audience accepts the fiction that the tale is told by the drunken Miller, while enjoying the elegance and subtlety of Chaucer's verse. An examination of lines 91–112 (the description of Nicholas) will make this clear; the narrative voice is clearly Chaucer's, not the Miller's. However, Chaucer does moderate his displays of learning to keep them within the compass of the uneducated Miller. His use of authorities and references is restricted, which also helps to keep the tale short.

Finally, the tale is a fabliau. These low-life tales are ideal for lowly characters such as the Miller and the Reeve; the fact that Chaucer also assigns one to the Merchant indicates his willingness to make free use of the genre in *The Canterbury Tales*.

Moral vision

The question of whether or not Chaucer has a moral purpose in 'The Miller's Tale' is hotly disputed. Many people interpret the tale as simply a highly enjoyable, bawdy romp suitable for a character like the Miller. Justice, if it is done at all, is of a fairly rough and ready sort — literally so in the case of Nicholas, and in the fact that naivety is rewarded with a broken arm. Alison escapes scot-free.

Other readers are not content with this. Given the place of the tale in the pilgrimage framework of *The Canterbury Tales*, some critics seek a more deliberate moral stance from Chaucer (if not from the Miller), and want to find a more cohesive moral plan for the *Tales* as a whole. An amoral, or even immoral, tale so early in the collection would apparently undermine the possibility of finding an overall moral message.

It is essential for you to decide for yourself whether the tale carries a moral meaning; this is not easy if you are studying 'The Miller's Tale' in isolation, and you must bear this limitation in mind when forming your judgement. At the end of the *Tales*, in his famous 'Retraction', Chaucer includes the biblical quotation, 'Al that is written is written for oure doctrine'; that is to say, 'Everything written has been composed for our learning'. This is a shortened version of 2 Timothy 3:16 in the

New Testament: 'All scripture is given by inspiration of God, and is profitable for doctrine, for reproof, for correction, for instruction in righteousness.'

The relevance of Chaucer's 'Retraction'

It is important to distinguish between the expectations of modern and medieval audiences here. In general, a modern audience does not enjoy being preached at, and if it is going to be instructed by art, it prefers that the instruction is implicit rather than explicit. Modern readers are accustomed to there often being a separation between entertainment and instruction, and so will frequently tend to view Chaucer as primarily entertainment.

However, a medieval audience would have been used to being preached at — literally. Art usually had a religious function, and serious literature would be expected to carry moral authority. Chaucer's original audience would have been far more aware of the moral and religious implications of what it heard, and far more knowledgeable about the religious details and references contained in *The Canterbury Tales*. It would certainly have been alert to the satirical qualities of the tale, and might have interpreted it in a more serious religious fashion without devaluing its comic effect. The modern audience therefore has to work a lot harder than its medieval counterpart to appreciate the moral values communicated in such an ostensibly bawdy piece. You are encouraged to adopt something of a medieval mindset if you are to appreciate the tale properly.

'The Miller's Tale' as a religious work

The best account of a truly scriptural reading is given by D. W. Robertson in *A Preface to Chaucer* (Princeton University Press, 1962), where he concludes: 'It should be emphasised that the scriptural ideas in this story in no way detract from its humor; on the contrary, the humorous as opposed to the merely **farcical** element in it is due entirely to its theological background' (p. 386).

A more limited version of this argument will serve, however. It is possible to see the tale as containing warnings against the **seven deadly sins**, particularly avarice (the desire for possessions, in this case Alison herself) and lust (at which all the characters excel). This is linked to 'The Parson's Tale', with its sermon on the sins and how to avoid them. The mock version of the Flood can be viewed as a cautionary tale, with the concluding lines showing how the characters learn their lessons: 'The false flood in this instance effects a purification, just as the original flood did, albeit on a very small scale' (Robertson, ibid).

'The Miller's Tale' as a moral work

It is easy to argue that the tale achieves some of the purposes indicated in the quotation from 2 Timothy given above. It is a satire, and the purpose of satire is to hold folly or vice up to ridicule, usually with the intention of alerting a reader to it

or condemning it in some way. In this tale none of the characters emerge with credit, and they do not need to be punished for the reader to appreciate that the behaviour of all the characters is either foolish (John and Absolon) or reprehensible (Nicholas and Alison).

The tale is about marriage, and the inappropriate match of John and Alison and its almost inevitable consequences. In this sense it forms part of the overall portrayal of marriage that some critics have seen as a unifying principle in *The Canterbury Tales*.

'The Miller's Tale' as entertainment

Of course the tale can be enjoyed on a simple level as mere entertainment, and doubtless this accounts for its enduring popularity as one of the favourite and best-known of Chaucer's tales. The comment by Chaucer the pilgrim in 'The Miller's Prologue' (lines 59–78) should be taken into account, with his pretence that he is merely repeating what he has heard, but it is mere authorial posturing, excusing the inclusion of a risqué tale. It has little bearing on the intentions of the author, who has of course deliberately placed the tale at this point in his scheme.

However, the whole of *The Canterbury Tales* can be described as entertainment, as can any literary work, including *Hamlet* and *Paradise Lost*. To label the tale as merely entertaining loses any sense of its complexity, and reduces it to a superficial reading that you are unlikely to find satisfying in the end.

Chaucer's narrative technique

'The Miller's Tale' is a masterpiece of narrative technique. Chaucer interweaves three plots — the love affair of Nicholas and Alison, the fooling of John with the story of the flood, and Absolon's failed attempt to woo Alison. In this way Chaucer (and the Miller) can gain considerable momentum, moving the narrative forward at a brisk pace to maintain the audience's attention. Curiously, this is at odds with many medieval narratives (including several of *The Canterbury Tales*), in which long digressions and examples are commonplace and apparently popular, although they are rarely to modern taste.

'The Miller's Tale' has no significant digressions from the central plots and no reliance on long citations from authorities, such as can be found in 'The Wife of Bath's Tale' and 'The Merchant's Tale'. The nearest it gets is the descriptions of Alison in lines 125–62 and Absolon in lines 204–30. Otherwise, almost the whole tale is a genuine narrative that tells a story, the passages of dialogue serving to develop the sequence of events.

It is notable that, while the story of the love affair is intertwined with each of the other two plots, there is no real interaction between Absolon and John. This

maintains clarity. The single occasion when John is aware of Absolon (lines 256–61) is left undeveloped, which avoids confusion between the plot strands.

It is not until the final part of the tale, from line 535 onwards, that the three strands of narrative come together. It is while Nicholas and Alison are in bed together that Absolon arrives, and the business with the ploughshare is the immediate cause of John's awakening and fall from the ceiling. The word 'water' in lines 707 and 709 neatly and satisfyingly connects the separate narrative threads, and precipitates the climax of the tale.

As always, it is important to keep in mind that the narrative skill is Chaucer's, not the Miller's. There is no pretence that the Miller has the ability to create such a well-paced and multi-stranded story.

Speech and dialogue

Approximately 40% of the tale is speech and dialogue, with the main characters divided as follows:

Nicholas	107 lines
John	49 lines
Alison	26 lines
Absolon	55 lines

It is notable that Alison speaks relatively little — her function is to be the focus of attention for the three men, not to express her own opinions and ideas. The only extended speech is by Nicholas in lines 418–92, where he is expounding the details of his incredible plan to the credulous John. Otherwise the dialogue tends to be in short snatches intended to drive the narrative forward, as in lines 169–92, which covers the entire wooing process between Nicholas and Alison.

Despite the restriction of the rhyming couplet form, Chaucer's command of colloquial dialogue is one of his most striking and well-known attributes. He creates both extended speeches and realistic conversation with equal ease. Look for example at the following:

- Absolon's interior monologue (lines 564–78)
- the mock seriousness of Nicholas's speech (lines 393–99) and the naturalistic manner of John's reply (lines 400–04)
- the colloquialisms in lines 631–38

Literary terms and concepts

Assessment Objective 1 requires 'insight appropriate to literary study, using appropriate terminology'. A knowledge of literary terms is therefore essential for A-level literature students, and allows responses to texts to be worded precisely and concisely. The terms and concepts below have been selected for their relevance to the study of 'The Miller's Prologue and Tale'.

allegory	extended metaphor which veils a moral, religious or political underlying meaning
alliteration	repetition of initial letter or sound in adjacent words to create an atmospheric or onomatopoeic effect, e.g. 'maiden meke' ('The Miller's Tale', line 94)
ambiguity	capacity of words to have two meanings in the context as a device for enriching meaning
analogy	perception of similarity between two things
apostrophe	direct address to a divinity, object or abstract concept, such as Freedom
archetype	original model used as recurrent symbol, e.g. the Flood
assonance	repetition of vowel sound in words in close proximity
bathos	sudden change of register from the sublime to the ridiculous
bawdy	lewd; with coarse, humorous references to sex
blazon	device in medieval poetry whereby a woman's body is described and celebrated in close detail
caricature	exaggerated and ridiculous portrayal of a person built around a specific physical or personality trait, e.g. John and his jealousy
characterisation	means by which fictional characters are personified and made distinctive
climax	moment of intensity to which a series of events has been leading
colloquial	informal language of conversational speech
contextuality	historical, social and cultural background of a text
couplet	two consecutive lines of poetry that are paired in rhyme

courtly love	in the Middle Ages a code governing the behaviour of aristocratic lovers, with a subservient lover adoring an idealised woman
criticism	evaluation of literary text or other artistic work
denouement	unfolding of the final stages of a plot, when all is revealed
dialogue	direct speech of characters engaged in conversation
didactic	with the intention of teaching the reader and instilling moral values
elements	earth, air, fire, water, of which it was believed in the Middle Ages that the universe was composed, with corresponding humours to explain human temperament
empathy	identifying with a character in a literary work
end-stopped	line of poetry which ends with some form of punctuation, creating a pause
enjamb(e)ment	run-on instead of end-stopped line of poetry, usually to reflect meaning
epicurean	devoted to luxury and self-indulgence
epithet	recurring characteristic adjective affixed to a name, e.g. 'hende Nicholas', line 91
fabliau	short medieval tale in rhyme, of a coarsely comic and satirical nature
farce	improbable and absurd dramatic events to excite laughter
figurative	using imagery; non-literal use of language
genre	type or form of writing with identifiable characteristics, e.g. fairy tale, fabliau
heroic couplet	iambic pentameter rhymed in pairs; traditional form of classical epic poetry
humours	four bodily fluids produced by different organs and related to one of the elements, an excess of which caused particular temperaments: yellow bile (anger), blood (happiness), phlegm (calmness), black bile (melancholy)
iambic pentameter	five feet of iambs, i.e. unstressed/stressed alternating syllables
imagery	descriptive language appealing to the senses; imagery may be sustained or recurring throughout texts, usually in the form of simile or metaphor

irony	a discrepancy between the actual and implied meaning of language; or an amusing or cruel reversal of an outcome expected, intended or deserved; situation in which one is mocked by fate or the facts
juxtaposition	placing side by side for (ironic) contrast of interpretation
legend	story about historical figures which exaggerates their qualities or feats
metaphor	suppressed comparison implied not stated, e.g. when Absolon addresses Alison as 'my sweete cinamome' line 591)
metre	regular series of stressed and unstressed syllables in a line of poetry
myth	fiction involving supernatural beings which explains natural and social phenomena and embodies traditional and popular ideas
narrative	connected and usually chronological series of events that form a story
parody	imitation and exaggeration of style for purpose of humour and ridicule
pathos	evocation of pity by a situation of suffering and helplessness
plot	cause-and-effect sequence of events caused by characters' actions
register	level of formality of expression
rhetoric	art of persuasion using emotive language and stylistic devices, e.g. triple structures, rhetorical questions
rhyme	repetition of final vowel sound in words at the end of lines of poetry
rhythm	pace and sound pattern of writing, created by metre, vowel length, syntax and punctuation
romance	story of love and heroism, deriving from medieval court life and fairy tale
satire	exposing vice or foolishness of a person or institution to ridicule
scansion	system of notation for marking stressed (/) and unstressed (~) syllables in a line of metrical verse
seven deadly sins	according to the medieval Catholic Church, the following sins were mortal and led straight to Hell: pride, envy, anger, sloth, avarice, gluttony, lust

simile	comparison introduced by 'as' or 'like', e.g. 'Hir month was sweete as bragot or the meeth' (line 153)
stereotype	category of person with typical characteristics, often used for mockery
syntax	arrangement of grammar and word order in sentence construction
theme	abstract idea or issue explored in a text
tone	emotional aspect of the voice of a text, e.g. 'And on his lippe he gan for anger bite' (Absolon, line 637)
wit	intelligent verbal humour

Questions & Answers

LITERATURE

Essay questions, specimen plans and notes

This section includes a range of essay questions on 'The Miller's Prologue and Tale', together with examining board material to help you understand what the examiners are looking for. Examinations may be 'open book', where you are permitted to take a copy of the text (normally with your own annotations) into the examination, or 'closed book', where you are not permitted the text in the examination. Note that at A-level students are expected to use accurate quotations to support points, so for a closed book examination you will need to learn as many quotations as you are likely to need. Quotations from Chaucer should always be given in the original Middle English, not in modernised form or paraphrase.

Passage-based questions: prescribed

A question of this type will direct you to a particular extract from the text. It will ask a specific question about the passage, but also ask you to place the extract in the context of the whole text. Examiners advise that a substantial portion (up to 60%) of responses to passage-based questions should refer to the rest of the work being studied. Answers that only deal with the specified extract are likely to be heavily penalised. Focus closely on the passage(s) but also relate its content and/or language to elsewhere in the text, backwards and forwards, and link your comments to the overall themes and/or structure of the text. Start by placing the passage in its context and summarising the situation. Include references to character, event, theme and language, and ask how the episode modifies or adds to our understanding so far, and how typical it is of the work as a whole.

1 **Remind yourself of lines 493–548 (from 'This sely carpenter goth forth his wey' to 'And freres in the chauncel gonne singe'), in which John carries out the instructions given by Nicholas. What is the importance of this section in the context of the whole of 'The Miller's Prologue and Tale'?**

Focus: lines 493–548, whole text.
Key words: what is the importance, this section, context of whole prologue and tale.
AOs: 1–3, 5i

Top band criteria
- conceptual exploration using relevant critical vocabulary
- sophisticated analysis of Chaucer's techniques
- confident analysis of this section's importance within an overview of the whole prologue and tale

(Source: AQA(A) Unit 3, January 2004)

2 Remind yourself of lines 113–62 (from 'This carpenter hadde wedded newe a wyf' to 'Or yet for any good yeman to wedde'), in which the Miller describes the carpenter's marriage and his wife. What do you find interesting about this portrayal of a fourteenth-century woman?

Possible ideas to include in a plan
- the conventional situation – older man, younger woman
- the idea of a woman as a possession
- conventional/stereotypical elements of the description of Alison
- individual elements in the description – her 'animal' magnetism
- how little has changed between medieval and modern times

3 Read lines 379–429 from 'The Miller's Tale' then answer all the questions.
(a) What does Nicholas explain to John and what is John's response?
(b) How are the characters of Nicholas and John reflected in their speech?
(c) How is deceit presented here and in the tale as a whole?

Focus: (a) understanding of Nicholas's and John's words; (b) illustration of how words reflect character; (c) some discussion of examples of deceitful behaviour.
AOs: 2i, 3

Possible content
(a) Nicholas predicts another flood; John is credulous but concerned mostly about Alison.
(b) Ingenuity and dominance from Nicholas; credulity and submissiveness from John.
(c) Deceit in Nicholas and Alison; self-deception in John and Absolon.

Top band criteria
AO2i   Secure conceptual knowledge/understanding of the text with full support.
AO3   Recognition of technique and features of form, structure and language.
AO3   Commentary on how form, structure and language shape meanings.
(Source: AQA(B) Unit 2, January 2003)

Further questions
4 Read lines 244–90 from 'The Miller's Tale' then answer all the questions.
(a) How is the character of Absolon presented here?
(b) Comment on the humorous aspects of the situation.
(c) Comment on the significance of this passage in the context of the whole tale.
5 Read lines 326–81 from 'The Miller's Tale' then answer all the questions.
(a) Comment on John's reaction to what his servant tells him.
(b) Comment on the humour in the passage.
(c) Show how this passage sets up Nicholas's plan to deceive the carpenter in the rest of the tale.

6 Remind yourself of lines 579–633 (from 'Whan that the firste cok hath crowe, anon' to 'And Absolon gooth forth a sory pas'), in which John carries out the instructions given by Nicholas. What is the importance of this section in the context of the whole of 'The Miller's Prologue and Tale'?

Whole-text questions

Underline the key words in the question and ensure that you address them thoroughly. Look out for questions asking you 'how' Chaucer achieves effects or 'why' he includes particular details. Unless the question is given in bullet points the structure of the essay is entirely your responsibility, and you should take special care in planning your work before you start.

1 In 'The Miller's Prologue', Chaucer informs us that the Miller 'tolde his cherles tale in his manere'. Explore the ways that the Miller's character is reflected in 'The Miller's Tale'.

Focus: whole text, Miller's character.

Key words: 'tolde his cherles tale in his manere', explore the ways, Miller's character reflected in tale.

AOs: 1–3, 5i

Top band criteria

- sophisticated analysis founded on mastery of the text
- cogent argument with mature expression
- confident exploration of the presentation of the Miller and its reflection within the context of the tale

(Source: AQA(A) mark scheme, January 2004)

2 What is the importance of Alison in the Tale?

Possible ideas to include in a plan

- her symbolic significance as an object of temptation for all three men
- her realistic presence, e.g. her physical description
- her behaviour towards each of the other characters – the moral dimension
- her function within the plot to deceive John
- the Miller's portrayal of women
- Chaucer's portrayal of women

Further questions

3 What interests you about Chaucer's presentation of relationships between women and men in 'The Miller's Tale'?

4 'The tale told by the Miller is rich in ironic effects.' Consider your view of 'The Miller's Tale' in the light of this comment.

5 'The Miller's Tale' has been described as 'setting personal pleasure against spiritual values'. How helpful do you find this description to your understanding of the tale and its effects?

6 How far do you agree that in 'The Miller's Tale' Chaucer does not judge wickedness but is simply amused by it?

7 'Self-deception is the most important theme in the 'The Miller's Tale'.' How far do you agree with this reading of the poem?

Practice questions

These questions are an additional resource. They are designed to be used as practice at any stage of your study of the text. Some are suitable for brief answers as well as more extended essays.

1 Is the essential tone of 'The Miller's Prologue and Tale' morally serious or comic?

2 Discuss the effects of the way Chaucer introduces the character of Alison to the reader. Look closely at how language, descriptive detail and imagery create an impression.

3 Which do you think is the most admirable or least admirable of the characters in 'The Miller's Tale'? How does their portrait relate to the moral values of the medieval world?

4 How does Chaucer create interest and humour in 'The Miller's Tale'?

5 Can 'The Miller's Tale' be viewed as antifeminist?

6 Comment on what the portraits in 'The Miller's Tale' suggest about attitudes towards the church in Chaucer's time.

7 Turn to the ending of 'The Miller's Tale', beginning at line 690. How satisfactory an ending do you consider this to be, bearing in mind all that has gone before in the tale?

8 Chaucer's irony is not always kindly and tolerant. Choose two passages in 'The Miller's Tale' where you think he conveys strong disapproval and show how he achieves this effect.

9 Lines 91–112 describe Nicholas; lines 113–24 describe the carpenter; lines 125–62 describe the carpenter's wife. How does Chaucer, through his descriptive devices in these lines, excite your anticipation for the story that is to follow?

10 Someone once described 'The Miller's Tale' as a rude story told with speed and wit. To what extent do you agree?

11 How does Chaucer's use of everyday life and domestic detail contribute to the overall impact of 'The Miller's Tale'?

12 Discuss the symbolic implications of the references to the Flood in 'The Miller's Tale'.

13 Write about the importance of Nicholas in 'The Miller's Tale'. Examine the ways in which Chaucer presents this character, and explore his contribution to the development of the plot.

14 Write about the importance of John the Carpenter, paying particular attention to his contribution to the humour of 'The Miller's Tale'.

15 Comment on Chaucer's presentation of Absolon and his significance in the story.

16 How far do you feel that the personality of the Miller has influenced his tale?

Sample essays

Below are two sample student essays, both falling within the top mark band. You can judge them against the Assessment Objectives for this text for your exam board and decide on the mark you think each deserves, and why. You may see ways in which each could be improved in terms of content, style and accuracy.

Sample essay 1

Remind yourself of lines 91–146 (from 'This clerk was cleped hende Nicholas' to 'So gay a popelote or swich a wenche'), in which the Miller introduces the tale's main characters. What is the importance of this section in the context of the whole of 'The Miller's Prologue and Tale'?

In a mere 50 lines the Miller not only vividly introduces three of the four central characters in his tale, but also sets the scene and gives background information for the comedy that will follow.

In a basic sense, the passage serves to introduce the central characters, and it is immediately evident that there is a traditional love triangle. Attention is focused on the young lovers, Nicholas and Alison, but the figure of John the carpenter looms large in the situation.

The Miller carefully rations out his attention and degree of detail according to the attractiveness and interest of the characters for the audience. Alison is fully and physically described: 'As any wezele hir body gent and smal'; 'Ful smale ypulled were hire browes two'. This obsession with her physical attributes extends for a full 40 lines, with emphasis on her mouth, which is 'sweete as bragot or the meeth', and ending with the conclusion that she is a 'piggesnie', 'For any lord to leggen in his bedde'. Her clothes are also described in meticulous detail ('hir smok…broiden al bifoore/And eek bihinde, on hir coler aboute'), so that the audience has the fullest and most vivid impression of her as a desirable sex object.

By contrast, Nicholas is not physically described at all, although he is clearly attractive: 'he himself as sweete as is the roote/Of licoris'. The emphasis with him is laid on his knowledge and learning: 'His Almageste, and bookes grete and smale'. He is 'sleigh and ful prive', but he is also 'hende', and the reciprocal attraction between him and Alison is easy to understand.

Against this magnetism is set the carpenter. He receives the shortest treatment, but the words used to describe him are ample to set up the scenario for the tale. He is 'Jalous', 'old', and, crucially, 'his wit was rude'. Physically he is no match for Alison; mentally he is no match for Nicholas. His fate is sealed before the plot gets under way, which is why the tale is a comedy and not a tragedy. In the context of the whole prologue and tale, the audience's interest is not in the question of whether disaster will happen (tragedy), but how an easily predicted event will be worked out (comedy).

The Miller sandwiches the carpenter between the descriptions of Nicholas and Alison, and this merely heightens the weakness of his situation and the distinctions between him and them. Most obviously, 'she was wilde and yong, and he was old'. Moreover, he already 'demed himself been lik a cokewold', and there is neither surprise nor pity from the audience when he is duly cuckolded. He deserves it. The Miller makes this clear: 'Men sholde wedden after hire estaat', and even directly states that the carpenter has 'fallen in the snare'.

With such a beginning, there is only one course for the narrative to pursue, and the audience can sit back and enjoy it. The exact nature of the carpenter's downfall has also of course been carefully prepared, with the description of Nicholas's particular branch of knowledge. 'His astrelabie, longinge for his art' and the other arcane objects of his speciality (e.g. 'augrim stones') prepare us for the mumbo jumbo with which he deceives the carpenter into believing his nonsensical tale of a second flood: 'in myn astrologie,/As I have looked in the moone bright'. Similarly, the exact nature of the relationship between Nicholas and Alison has been prepared by her description. When the seduction scene comes, it is a crudely physical one: 'prively he caughte hire by the queynte'. There is no romance here, and the Miller is careful to avoid it; he doesn't want an overly sophisticated or empathic response to the situation of any of the characters.

It is a further tribute to the narrative art of the tale that the Miller (really, Chaucer) leaves out the character of Absolon from this opening sequence. Absolon will add a rich extra layer to the humour and comedy of the tale, and contribute a subplot in his forlorn wooing of Alison and its famously crude outcome ('Nicholas is scalded in the towte'), but he isn't a necessary character. The love triangle is the focus, a simple and traditional device to explore the behaviour (or misbehaviour) of human beings; the extra dimension offered by Absolon can wait until the main plot is fully established and clear. In fact, Absolon has to wait until line 204, nearly a third of the way through the tale, before he is introduced.

What Absolon does confirm, in keeping with the character of the Miller, is the strongly physical nature of much of the comedy in the tale. The farting, 'hir naked ers', the scalding and the carpenter's broken arm all have their origin in the lure of Alison's physicality. Nicholas's ingenuity underlies the plot to deceive the carpenter, but it is not the central

feature of the tale. That is why, right at the beginning, the Miller devotes so much time to describing Alison (lines 125–62), compared to the time devoted to Nicholas and John. The Miller may be a drunken buffoon, but Chaucer grants him an ability to construct a story which is second to none.

Sample essay 2

Read lines 690–746 of 'The Miller's Tale', then answer all the questions.
(a) How does Chaucer present the downfall of the carpenter?
(b) How important is Absolon in this part of the tale?
(c) How does this ending form a fitting conclusion to the tale as whole?

The ending is vital in bringing all the aspects of the tale together and leaving the audience something to think about.

The downfall of the carpenter is presented entirely in comic terms, literally as a falling down. In my opinion, Chaucer is supremely clever in linking the scalding of Nicholas (the Absolon subplot) with the fall of John (the Flood subplot). Nicholas's cry of 'water! water!' wakes John, and he crashes down in the middle of the chaos – 'doun gooth al', both literally and metaphorically. We could sympathise with John at this moment ('For with the fal he brosten hadde his arm'), but Chaucer doesn't give us the chance – Nicholas and Alison 'tolden every man that he was wood', and so 'The folk gan laughen at his fantasie'. It is obvious that Chaucer expects and wants the reader to laugh at him too – he has been so stupid and so gullible that he deserves what he gets.

The same is true of Absolon, and I think it is essential that he, like John, receives his comeuppance at the end of the tale. He has resembled John in many ways – the same kind of self-blindness and self-obsession makes them both ridiculous. In the same way that John gets a broken arm as a reward for his simplicity, so Absolon receives a fart 'As greet as it had been a thonder-dent', and again there is no sympathy from the reader. Anybody who goes around addressing a married woman as 'My fair brid, my sweete cinamone' deserves everything he gets in my opinion. The rough justice meted out to John and Absolon is parallel and merited, so Absolon is vital at this point in the narrative to point up the comparison (it's notable that he isn't mentioned after line 702 except in the conclusion).

Absolon is equally necessary as the agent for the similarly rough justice handed out to Nicholas ('amidde the ers he smoot'). We may have sided with Nicholas during the tale, enjoying his successful duping of John and the hilariously elaborate tale he spins ('And thanne shul we be lordes al oure lyf/Of al the world, as Noe and his wyf'), but there is no doubt that he deserves punishment as much as anybody. Vengeance is to come, and Absolon is on his way to dispense it.

It has often been remarked that, in this wonderfully immoral tale, Alison seems to escape scot-free, while all the men are humiliated and ridiculed. In examining the suitability of the conclusion of the tale, we have to deal with this issue. Chaucer appears to include her in the list of punishments in the last 5 lines ('Thus swived was this carpenteris wyf'),

but for most modern readers this doesn't appear a punishment at all. It is, after all, what she was after, in contrast to the misfortunes that befall the men.

I think that in order to get a fair sense of Chaucer's purpose we have to look at the tale from a medieval perspective. Adultery was a sin – lechery was a mortal sin – and so the fact that Alison has been adulterous is in itself a punishment – she's done wrong and has to be judged in terms of that. John may be a foolish and stupid husband, but the fact is that he is her husband, and she should not have married him unless she meant to be faithful. In the final analysis, her punishment is as physical as that of the others – she bears the stain of being an adulteress (even if the neighbours never discover the truth). I am aware that some people will not agree with this reading, but it gives a satisfying unity to the end of the tale that might otherwise be lacking.

Apart from this, the ending of 'The Miller's Tale' is an absolutely fitting conclusion to all that has gone before. It is satisfying in narrative terms – all the plot threads are neatly tied up (another reason why Absolon is so important here). It is satisfying in character terms – all the characters have something to remember their experiences by! And it is satisfying in simple moral terms – they have all learned their lesson, and it is unlikely that any of them will be so gullible again. The fact that the future relationship of John and Alison is left open is unimportant – it is the lesson learned at this point in their lives which matters.

All in all the ending of 'The Miller's Tale' is a comic masterpiece, genuinely funny, satis-fyingly neat, and not labouring under some heavy theological point that would weigh it down.

Further study

Complete editions

The standard edition is still F. N. Robinson's *The Works of Geoffrey Chaucer* (2nd edn), Oxford University Press (1957).

Larry D. Benson's 1988 edition of *The Riverside Chaucer* (Oxford University Press) is a convenient complete edition.

Modernised versions

Strictly speaking, it is wrong to use the word translation for Chaucer, as his work (like Shakespeare's) is written in English, albeit Middle English. These are really modernisations, but the word translation is often used.

The best known are the verse renderings by Nevill Coghill (Penguin) and David Wright (Oxford World's Classics). While these give a flavour of Chaucer for the non-specialist, a prose version is more suitable for studying, because it allows direct comparison with the original text. The recommended work is David Wright's prose modernisation of *The Canterbury Tales* (Fontana, 1996). Unfortunately, this omits the 'Tale of Melibee' and 'The Parson's Tale', but is otherwise the best way to read the complete *Tales*.

Readings

The easiest way to hear Chaucer's work read aloud is via the internet; there are a number of sites that offer extracts or complete tales, and some give pronunciation guides too. See the section on internet resources below. Libraries may have cassette tape or audio CD versions, e.g. the Penguin Audiobook version.

Background reading

There is a daunting number of books on Chaucer available; your school and local library will have a selection. It is worth looking out for the following:

Brewer, D. (1996) *Chaucer and His World*, Eyre Methuen. This is an excellent visual and biographical account of Chaucer. Derek Brewer has written and edited a number of accessible books on Chaucer.

Burrow, J. (1982) *Medieval Writers and Their Work: Middle English Literature and its Background 1100–1500*, Oxford University Press. This study places Chaucer in his literary context.

Rowland, B. (ed.) (1979) *Companion to Chaucer Studies*, Oxford University Press. This contains excellent essays on Chaucer and his background.

The internet

The internet is a marvellous source of material on Chaucer, because it permits the use of illustrations and sound in a way that not even the best books can match. There is also an enormous quantity of up-to-date material available, ranging from student guides to academic studies. A good search engine (Google is recommended) and the willingness to spend some time exploring will reveal considerable riches, and often unexpected and useful insights into all aspects of Chaucer's works, period and culture. Try the following starting points:

- www.unc.edu/depts/chaucer/index.html is the *Chaucer Metapage*, designed to offer links to many aspects of Chaucer.
- http://hosting.uaa.alaska.edu/afdtk/etc_genprol.htm contains *The Electronic Canterbury Tales* and a wealth of other information.
- www.luminarium.org/medlit/chaucer.htm is a good introduction to Chaucer.
- http://cla.calpoly.edu/~dschwart/engl512/gp.html has links to useful background material.
- www.mathomtrove.org/canterbury/links.htm is an excellent page of links to material on Chaucer and on the medieval background.
- www.courses.fas.harvard.edu/~chaucer/index.html includes an interactive guide to Chaucer's pronunciation, grammar and vocabulary, and interlinear modernisations of some of the tales.